LIVE THROUGH THIS

LIVE THROUGH THIS

SURVIVING THE INTERSECTIONS OF
SEXUALITY, GOD, AND RACE

CLAY CANE

Published in the United States by Cleis Press, an imprint of Start Midnight, LLC, 101 Hudson Street, Thirty-Seventh Floor, Suite 3705, Jersey City, NJ 07302.

Printed in the United States.
Cover design: Scott Idleman/Blink
Cover artist: Shawn K. Alexander
Text design: Frank Wiedemann
First Edition.
10 9 8 7 6 5 4 3 2 1

Trade paper ISBN: 978-1-62778-218-0
E-book ISBN: 978-1-62778-219-7

Library of Congress Cataloging-in-Publication Data is available on file.

TABLE OF CONTENTS

AUTHOR'S NOTE

THANK YOU FOR READING *LIVE THROUGH THIS: SURVIVING the Intersections of Sexuality, God, and Race.* This book is not a memoir, but a collection of essays. Each essay is a call to action for all of us to see beyond our own lens. *Live Through This* compounds personal narratives and societal analysis, but the interpretation is your own. The essays are a fusion of the humorous, campy, disturbing, heartbreaking, and inspirational. Moreover, the book is a cathartic journey of progression and reinvention, flourishing along the spectrum of lightness and darkness. I am deeply grateful for the platform to tell these stories. I fought for my voice with every step, but I fully own that I am privileged to unpack these experiences in a book.

As I grappled with various identities and survived hostile environments, in my lowest moments, I would ask: "Can I live through this?" I did. My lifeline for survival was understanding the nuances of race, class, gender, sexuality, and faith. My very being exists in intersectionality.

In this book I present harsh realities, which are often ignored by a society that pretends discrimination is a non-issue. Therefore, names, locations, and other minor details have been changed to protect identities. Most importantly, I am only speaking for myself, no one else. This book does not represent the stories of every black American, LGBT person, or black LGBT person. There are many more stories to be told; *Live Through This* is one of several beginnings.

As a writer, I believe language is crucial. However, the language I utilize may not be your choice. I rarely use the term "queer" to describe the spectrum of the lesbian, gay, bisexual, and transgender community. I prefer "LGBT," but I respect the verbiage that others choose to describe their own gender, sexual orientation, or identity. However, some of the language used in the essays might be shocking. In reality, life is shocking, and this is a book about life.

There are many people to thank: Nicole Ray, Antar Bush, Mae Andrews, Penny Thompson, Keith Boykin, Allen Orr, Monroe France, Rhonda Cowan, Shani Parrish, Lonnie Hopper, Ahesha Andrews, Jeremiah Jones,

Arin Perdue, Shawn K. Alexander, Christian John Wikane, Darnell L. Moore, Casinova Henderson, Torrence Glenn, Latoya Smith, Richard Sanders, Frederick Smith, Patrick Taliaferro, Barbara C. Foley, Ann Hlabangana-Clay, and Smriti Mundhra. Also, my literary agent, Dawn Michelle Hardy of Serendipity Literary Agency, and the entire teams at Serendipity Literary Agency and Cleis Press. Plus, all of the people I've encountered along the way: teachers, family, loved ones, coworkers, classmates, and friends. You made me better, pushing me to fight for my right to exist.

Lastly, this book is dedicated to two people. Alexa Munoz (since the river was young), the molecules in the room changed when we met and I haven't been the same since. I love you. To my mother, I survived and thrived because of your authenticity. Mom, this book is for you, you are immortalized now, I love you.

SEXUALITY

THE FIRST TIME
I WAS CALLED A
FAGGOT

GROWING UP, I WORSHIPPED ALL THINGS GIRLY. LIKE MANY other boys, I loved *Star Wars*, but in my mind, Princess Leia ran the show. I acted out elaborate scenarios in which she flipped the Jedi narrative and was the one who chained up Jabba the Hutt. I owned He-Man action figures, but when in possession of a black Barbie, whom I named Dee-Dee, order was finally in place and she became the real master of the universe. I once dyed my hair blonde, which turned into a strange orange color, but I didn't care—I was a blonde in my mind, lip-synching to Donna Summer's "On the Radio" in the closest mirror. Today, experts might politely, clinically describe my childhood expressions as "gender nonconforming," but back then I was a sissy, a punk, soft, and, of course, a faggot. All praise goes to my mom, who didn't grow up in a progressive home (or era), but for whatever reason, she let me exist. Creative freedom for a child was rare in those times. That said, I vividly remember the first time I was called a faggot. I was seven years old.

I loved watching my mother get dressed up. She was only eighteen when I was born, so when I was seven, she was a twenty-five-year-old woman who could still drop it like it was hot—whenever she could find and afford a babysitter. My mother's soundtrack was the pop and R&B of the 1980s: Madonna, Prince, George Michael, and Janet Jackson. I was mesmerized watching her prepare for a night on the town as she sang along to Klymaxx's "The Men All Pause" or Sheila E.'s "The Glamorous Life." She stood before the bathroom mirror, dolling herself up with the harsh beauty products of the 1980s: press-on nails, icy blue eye shadow, endless blush, and enough Aqua Net hairspray to clog your lungs. By the time she was finished, she had transformed herself into a fusion of *True Blue*-era Madonna and Wendy from Prince and the Revolution.

Fascinated by my mother's magic, naturally, I wanted to experience all this glamour for myself. So one fine evening, when she couldn't find a baby-sitter, I begged to dress up in her clothes. She huffed and puffed, but eventually gave in—I was a highly persuasive child. I knew instantly what I wanted to wear. I picked out a maraschino-red, bedazzled, sequined gown with a sweetheart neckline and more trim than a Christmas tree. I shimmied my tiny boy feet into spiked, black pumps. I felt like Donna Summer on the cover of the *Bad Girls* album! Although I was channeling more of a Cyndi Lauper vibe, the *She's So Unusual* era—but I digress. Of course I needed some makeup, and my mom helped me apply a little lipstick and a touch of eye shadow. I saw myself in the mirror and was overjoyed. I captured a bit of my mother's magic.

I was in a state of jubilation, running around our small apartment, screaming with excitement. My mother stared after me inquisitively, not with disappointment, or worse, judgment, but more with uncertainty. She didn't possess the language to describe what I was doing. This was the mid-1980s; the idea of gender nonconforming children wasn't on the radar. Yet, somewhere in her soul, my mother understood that I was simply playing with gender, exercising creativity.

In the midst of my joy, my mother's on-and-off boyfriend unexpectedly arrived. He was tall, masculine, played electric guitar, and spoke with a deep voice that often frightened me. My mother gave him a huge hug—they had recently reconciled. However, once he caught a glimpse of me in ill-fitting heels, a baggy red dress, and makeup on my face, his mouth twisted.

He snapped at my mother, nearly roaring, "You got your son in women's clothes! What the fuck is wrong with you?"

Knots tied in my stomach. Something was wrong. I was suddenly embarrassed by my mother's clothes. I was ashamed of the makeup. I began to fidget, wiping off the red lipstick with the back of my hand, but only managing to smudge it over my face.

"You got your son dressed like a girl?" he continued, his anger and shock flooding the apartment. "Your son is gonna be a faggot!"

That was my first time hearing the word, and I would hear it a million times after that, but this moment was vital. I was vulnerable and impressionable. My childhood imagination, innocence, and admiration of my mother's magic were at stake. I turned to Mommy, searching her face for what was next. She locked eyes with me. I was scared. Maybe she was scared, too. Maybe she regretted letting me play dress-up. Mother and son, we had reached a crucial fork in the road of my development. Whatever my mother did at that moment would either damage or affirm me for life. My little soul was in her hands.

Without hesitation, my twenty-five-year-old mother turned to her boyfriend and yelled with a voice as powerful as his and a presence even stronger, "This is *my* child! This is *my* son! He's being a kid!" She pointed to the door. "Get the *fuck* out of my house!" I never saw him again.

I've heard similar stories, but with terrible endings. Sometimes it's simply the disappointed look in a parent's eyes when a child goes against the repressive norm. Sometimes it is a young boy getting caught in his mom's clothes and being beaten till he bleeds. However, the day I first heard the word *faggot* spoken with such venom, I learned that my mother's love was stronger than bigotry, anger, and hate. I'm certain that if she hadn't chosen my happiness— and safety—over her own ambivalence in that moment, my life as a child in Washington State, and later as a teenager in 1990s Philadelphia and an adult in New York City, would have been strikingly different.

As time went on, my gender nonconformity faded, but my creativity as a writer flourished. My mother's encouragement to explore my self-expression—at any cost—continues to set me free in all of my intersecting identities. I still struggled, as a young gay man, to assert myself within the confines of traditional definitions of masculinity. I've been called everything from "faggot" to "nigger" to "spic," but that one moment of affirmation armored me for life. I've always felt a protective force field around me from that day when I was seven years old. I am eternally grateful to my young mother. She personified unconditional love and gave me agency in her red dress. When your mother loves you, when your mother affirms you, no one else matters.

2 POP LIFE

WHEN I WAS A CHILD, POP CULTURE, ESPECIALLY MUSIC, rescued me. In high school, as my sexuality was uncontrollably rising to the surface, I would cut class after lunch and ride the city bus for hours with my Sony Walkman, an extra pack of batteries, and countless cassettes stuffed in my backpack. I'd ride to neighborhoods I'd never been to, with big houses, lush green grass, and nuclear families sitting behind the windows. I was jealous of their bubble. I knew my life would never resemble that type of Americana, but my soundtrack inspired me on those bus rides, convincing me that I was capable of reinvention. No other artists had a bigger impact on me than Madonna and Prince.

My mother was a huge fan of His Royal Badness. Well, "fan" isn't the most fitting word; she was deeply obsessed with the 5'2" musical prodigy. Prince was her boyfriend, husband, lover, and addiction. The release of *Purple Rain* in June of 1984 was a major event in my house. I was seven in 1984, and my mother was twenty-five, still young and not totally over the fanatical years we all experience in our youth. These were the days before music streaming, album leaks, or YouTube. The sole way of hearing the latest music was camping out by the radio and praying for the deejay to play your favorite song.

My mother and her best friend, Karla, a Chicana woman who was the same age as her, both worshipped the Purple One. They were delirious with anticipation for the *Purple Rain* album. Word got out that there was a contest at our local radio station in Vancouver, Washington, and the first twenty people in line with purple balloons would win a copy of the album. My mother and Karla seriously prepared: dressed in head-to-toe purple—even their makeup. (Purple eye shadow and lipstick were extra, even in the 1980s). They made a beeline for the radio station early in the morning, but when they arrived, the line already wound around the block.

As legend has it, when Karla saw a small cart of *Purple Rain* albums pushed to the front of the line by one of the radio hosts, she screamed and charged uncontrollably through the line. Bulldozing her way through, with my mother right behind her, Karla wailed, terrifying people and accidentally smacking a batch of purple balloons into a random woman's face. Purple chaos ensued as everyone bolted to the front of the line, with my mom and Karla in the lead. They snatched their *Purple Rain* albums, screaming like they were on *The Price Is Right,* and ran back to the car. My mother said, "I'm surprised we didn't get arrested!"

When *Purple Rain* opened in theaters, my mother and Karla made it a full extravaganza. They saw the film countless times and argued over who looked more like Apollonia, Prince's girlfriend in the film. My mom consistently needed her purple fix, and when she couldn't find a babysitter, she dragged me along. When the smoky silhouette of Prince hit the screen, right on cue, my mother squeezed my hand, threw her other hand in the air, and screamed in the theater. I would whisper loudly, "Mommy, please stop! You're embarrassing me!"

But it didn't stop there. Every single solitary time Prince popped up on screen, she let out a holler, yelp, or something to the effect of, "Oh, Lord!" "I love him!" *"Priiiince!"*

"Mom!" I'd say, mortified. "This is his movie. He's gonna be in it the entire time!" I can't remember how many times I experienced *Purple Rain* on the big screen.

The *Purple Rain* album played on heavy rotation for the rest of the 1980s, in every house we ever lived in. Vinyl records were easily scratched, and my mother must've run through ten copies, getting her money's worth from each. In our lowest moments, when she had been laid off from another job, food was scarce, and we suffered the end-of-the-month hunger pangs, we'd dance together to "I Would Die 4 U," an invaluable three-minute escape. Her dedication to Prince extended to all of his protégés, especially Sheila E. Mom played *The Glamorous Life* ad nauseam. When she bought the album on cassette, we'd drive through the rich neighborhoods of Washington State, admiring all of the glamour. As Sheila E. pounded her drums, Mom would prophesize, "One day you're going to live the glamorous life, baby. One day."

There were pictures of three people on the walls of my home: Dr. Martin Luther King, Jr.; Jesus; and Prince—but it was clear who reigned supreme. My mother decorated our entire apartment with Prince albums—*Controversy* on the windowsill, *For You* on the kitchen table, and *1999* propped up by the television. Magazines, posters that had come with the albums, and clippings from newspapers—Prince was present in every corner of our home.

My first memory of Prince is a milestone in my life. I was mesmerized by the *Dirty Mind* album cover, which sat on the nightstand in my mother's bedroom. Prince stands seductively in skimpy black briefs, a bandana around his neck, rocking a trashy 1980s jacket with the springs of a mattress behind him. I was strangely attracted to the album cover, sneaking into my mother's bedroom to obsess over Prince's eyes, legs, and the pubic hair peeking out above his briefs. He triggered my sexuality. Yes, Prince officially made me gay. Blame it on Prince.

As I stared at Prince's eclectic album covers, I was fascinated by a man who, to my childhood brain, didn't present himself as the standard image of masculinity. He was gender nonconforming before the term existed. How could Prince be so effeminate and still be considered masculine? This was the question my underdeveloped mind attempted to process. My white mother and her Mexican best friend were lusting after a short and, for lack of a better word, *femme* man, who basically performed in drag. Plus, a little gay boy like me also felt an intense attraction. The Purple One's appeal was universal—he was beloved beyond race, nationality, gender, age, and sexual orientation. Prince completely fucked up my world, and I am forever thankful.

There was also the *Around the World in a Day* album, which was released in 1985. For hours, I would gaze at the cover, transfixed by the images of a woman with a condition of the heart, the young boy flying on a balloon, and the man in all black clutching his tambourine. I imagined that was exactly what Paisley Park, Prince's Minneapolis home, would be—a space of interconnecting stories.

Around the World in a Day is the first time I remember being sparked politically. Although they may be very young, even children can recognize societal imbalances. The song "America" shot through me as Prince critiqued God, country, and classism. In the era of the crack epidemic, the "war on drugs," HIV/AIDS, and Reaganomics, which pushed the country's national debt into the trillions, Prince made pointed observations of America. Beneath the guitars and godly vocal prowess, he was a musical activist for me, a Nina Simone with lace panties on his face.

Prince tapped into my angst as a child living under the lie of trickle-down economics, a clear attack on the poor. Poverty shames, and when you have no agency to express your rage, music is often your only outlet. This was especially true of my life in the 1980s. Prince's "America" resonated with every welfare check and block of government cheese my mother and I received. However, Prince's work was unpredictable. The Purple One wouldn't abandon you in anger, but would remix you into accountability. The next track after "America" is "Pop Life," where Prince turns the mirror on the listener, questioning if you are simply a victim of poverty.

I was confused. Was he now blaming the disenfranchised for their circumstances, cosigning a pull-yourself-up-by-your-bootstraps mentality? Not exactly. Prince challenged his listeners to take control. It's about ownership over your right to exist, which is a perfect description of today's movements: Black Lives Matter, LGBT equality, feminism, and the rights of the undocumented. In many ways, politics has become pop life; Prince saw that in his musical crystal ball. Pop is king. This is often not good—and may explain the madness of our last presidential election.

Around the World in a Day also tackled taboos. In songs like "Temptation," where a conflicted Prince conjoined God and sex as only he could do, his manic cries encouraged an exploration of sexuality that wasn't void of grace or faith. Sex and God were not mutually exclusive in Prince's world. The theme of "Temptation" reminded me of 1981's "Controversy," where he sang about sexuality, faith, and race. Black, white, straight, gay, and God—even as a toddler, that was my story. Prince made me feel not so alone; he appeared to understand me.

When I was a preteen—bullied, confused, and grappling with every identity imaginable—Madonna became my goddess. From the late 1980s to the mid-1990s, Madonna vexed America with her blunt presentations of sex, religion, gender, and even race. Seeing a black Jesus in the 1989 "Like a Prayer" video blew my world to pieces. One of my white, Christian neighbors attempted to convince me the video was demonic. My mother countered by telling me they were fanatical, Bible-beating racists and I wasn't allowed to be around their ignorance again.

Nineteen ninety-one's "Vogue" showed me a world I didn't know existed: black and Latin men, boldly gay, dancing, posing, and popping, while Madonna was relegated to the role of a costar. My mother would vogue with me, not knowing the roots of voguing or ballroom culture. Little did I know that five years later, I would dip into the ballroom scene, a subculture of LGBT people of color encompassing fashion, creativity, and dance. This is where voguing began. I found freedom in voguing with my mother. When someone from school babbled that Madonna revealed voguing was a form of dance she saw in the gay community, and if I vogued I was a fag, I ran home and told my mother. She answered, "Don't let anybody stop you from dancing. You vogue, do the running man, whatever the hell you want." While Madonna is often critiqued for cultural misappropriation, as a child, I never saw an outward expression of black and Latin LGBT culture from any other mainstream artist except for Madonna. Her work was a vessel to clearly see myself. And then there was the documentary about 1990's Blond Ambition tour, *Truth or Dare*.

Most gay men will tell you about the impact of seeing two men kiss for the first time. For me, it was Madonna's two dancers—who were boyfriends— passionately and deeply kissing on screen after a dare from Madge. Their long, deep tongue kiss traveled leagues beyond the untapped sexuality that had been sparked in me by Prince's *Dirty Mind* album cover. This was a clear presentation of two men, one of color, sharing affection. There was no censoring, no shame, and no mocking. Madonna added, "I'm getting a hard-on!" As did I— at fourteen, I credit Madonna for the first teenage erection I can remember.

For most of my childhood and teenage years, I was a Madonna encyclopedia. My favorite story of the Queen of Pop was this: In 1979, she dropped out of the University of Michigan, moved to New York City with thirty-five dollars in her pocket, and told the cab driver to drop her off in the middle of everything. She landed in Times Square, and the rest is pop culture history. For me, the City of Brotherly Love lacked the resources I needed to accomplish my dreams. I wanted to do something creative with my life; the concrete jungle called loud and clear. While visiting a friend in New York City in July of 1997, I sat in the food court at the Manhattan Mall and predicted, "I will be living in New York by August of next year." Nearly everyone told me that moving to New York would be a massive mistake, but I thought of Madonna's story. I was no Madge, but I felt like if she did it, I could at least try.

By early summer of 1998, I was on a crazed hunt for a job in Gotham. I wanted out of Philly and didn't quite have the gumption to travel with just thirty-five dollars like Madge, but my ambition was unstoppable. These were the days before online job searches, so every morning I walked to the only newsstand in my Philadelphia neighborhood that sold the *New York Times* and the *Village Voice*. I waded through endless job listings, searching for any gig that would take me. I spent tons of money faxing my resumé from local delis, believing that someone would bite if I kept the bait out long enough.

In July of 1998, I received a last-minute call from a temp agency to be at an interview in New York City by four p.m. It was noon when I got the call. I jumped on the next train and arrived at the temp agency's Midtown office fifteen minutes early. The woman who interviewed me said, "It's funny—I know people who live in Harlem and they can't get here on time. You're from Philly and you're here early!" The temp agency landed me a job at a cellular phone company, making just a few dollars above minimum wage, but I didn't care. It was my only option. Everything in my soul told me I needed to be in the orbit of New York City. I soon found a roach-infested one-bedroom apartment, which represented independence in my mind. On August 16, 1998—Madonna's birthday—at twenty-one years old, I sped down the New Jersey Turnpike, in a rental, singing my soul out to Madge's *Ray of Light* album, ready for Gotham City. Madonna inspired me to take the risk, and her music was my soundtrack against the fear and naysayers.

My liberation cannot be credited to pop stars. That work comes from within, but we all need inspiration, a beacon to get us through. It's hard to deny the need for your story to be represented, even if the messages or vessels require adjustments. However, I dismiss the notion that every community needs exact representation to see beyond their circumstances. If that was the case, I'd still be a closeted black man in West Philadelphia. Sometimes you have to remix the representations to work for your own narrative; there are rarely exact matches. Madonna and Prince are privileged pop stars who were far removed from the struggles of the average person by the time I connected to their work. Nonetheless, for me, whether it was sex, God, race, or class, their pop life brilliantly manifested pieces of my story in their art. These two pop icons unknowingly gave me freedom to exist in the deepest sense of myself—at any cost.

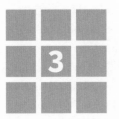

THIRTEENTH STREET

THE NIGHT BURNED AS I STOOD ON LOCUST AND
Thirteenth Streets in Center City, Philadelphia. The strip, as we called it, was an overcrowded world that oozed fantasies and dying dreams. Street lamps glowed as personalities packed together on corners, fighting for center stage in a civil war for attention. Authentic and bogus characters battled, destroying the delicate balance of gender and sexual roles. The belly of this world breathed stories of rejection and acceptance, anguish and reinvention. The life of the strip engrossed me. Cars drove down the badly paved roads, their drivers yelling at friends or a possible date. Young and old congregated on the sidewalks, masculine and feminine men and women wrapped around each other laughing and hugging. Music blasted from double-parked cars as bodies performed their own dances to the intense rhythms. My heart pounded; amazed I was among all these gay people of color. All my life I had associated gayness with whiteness.

"Why are you just standing there?" Nikki, my best friend, asked. It was June of 1995, the first Friday after I graduated from high school, and I promised Nikki that I would join her on Thirteenth Street—after midnight. The stories Nikki told me about Thirteenth Street were legendary. You could be whatever you wanted, exist on any spectrum, regardless of how you presented. I was still struggling with my sexuality, but Nikki didn't care if I was straight or gay; her consistent goal was for me and everyone around her "get your mothafuckin' life!" The strip was her world. A tall, graceful, voluptuous girl with godly rhythm, Nikki was an emotional and spiritual powerhouse, a classic fit for Thirteenth Street.

Nikki simultaneously rejected and embraced labels. "Honey," Nikki would say, "I ain't a dyke and I ain't straight cunt—I'm open to suggestions!" Then she'd declared, "I'm a faggot, always will be! Being a faggot makes you smart—it also makes you old!" Nikki's one-liners never failed to elicit responses of "I know that's right, bitch!" from our tribe on Thirteenth Street. Nikki was instrumental in helping me shed fear of my own sexuality. On Thirteenth Street, I wasn't concerned about straight people. Outside of the strip, heterosexuals were always analyzing me at work, school, and even on the streets. Paranoia made me wonder, "Do they think I'm gay?"—even when I had convinced myself that I wasn't gay. Yet, there I was on Thirteenth Street free from those thoughts, naturally comfortable, and among young people who appeared to exist in a freedom I never knew. People talked with their hands and bodies as if a sentence didn't sound right without over-expressive mannerisms to accompany the words. Fashion norms were annihilated with men and women wearing whatever matched their soul at the moment, and not whatever matched their so-called gender. Nikki continued to ask if I was okay, but I was in perfect awe.

Nikki was clearly a local celebrity; "the kids," as we were called, lived for "Miss Nikki." Her roots were Thirteenth Street, which she had been walking since she was fifteen years old. Nikki always told me, "Gay men taught me to love myself as a woman. They affirmed me. They loved me without sex. As a woman, I needed that from men. Gay men were the first men to love me without abusing me." Seeing Nikki in her element made me realize she had always been her authentic self since I met her in the tenth grade. Being with Nikki on the strip was identical to sitting in a classroom with her. When you looked into her eyes, you saw more than an eighteen-year-old. Like many black girls, Nikki was forced to be strong and exude "black girl magic," even when she didn't have magic in her. However, Nikki consistently emanated bold energy; she was a product of Thirteenth Street. Everything and everyone was bold, from the voices to the music and even the cars moving down the road.

As Nikki and I made our way down the strip, I saw a tall, strikingly beautiful woman strutting toward us. I wondered if she was Nikki's type. She had a near-perfect honey-almond complexion, dark eyes, and jet-black, micro-braided hair framing a stunning, soft face. She adjusted a bra strap under a tight-fitting navy blue dress that was a little too fancy for the middle of the night in downtown Philadelphia.

"What's up, Miss Deidra?" Nikki said, giving her an air kiss on the cheek.

"Nothing, child, getting ready to pop in the club," she answered in a raspy voice.

"All right girl, I'll see you in there later," Nikki replied.

"She was beautiful," I commented as we continued walking.

"Yes, she *is*, in every way. She is the Janet Jackson of Thirteenth Street. Kind of sad though; the kids only live for the femme queens when they look like her."

"Femme queen?" I heard Nikki use the term before, but I never understood what it meant. "What does that mean?"

"Do you pay attention to anything I say?" Nikki laughed. "Deidra used to be a boy, and now she is who she really is, a girl." These were the days before words like *transgender* and *cisgender* were commonly used, and before the understanding that someone like Deidra was never a "boy"—that was simply the gender she was assigned at birth. "That's what we call a femme queen."

I looked at Nikki questioningly. This felt like the safest place in the world, where everybody was affirmed. *Why did girls who didn't look as gorgeous as Deidra not get the same respect?* I thought. "There's no 100 percent safe place for femme queens," Nikki continued. "And really, there is no 100 percent safe place for us. We're the bottom of the barrel. We're black, gay, and whatever else. So we gotta fight even harder. Remember that, doll baby. Anyway, we gotta make it to the club!"

This was my first realization that Thirteenth Street was a fantasy, and even within the bubble, there were flaws. A woman like Deidra was praised on the strip, but other transgender women, who didn't fit cisgender norms, were dismissed. Even on Thirteenth Street, there were regulations. For example, a transgender woman couldn't present as even mildly masculine; she was expected to be "pussy," soft and feminine. No trace of her "boy" self was acceptable. Trans women were expected to perform the role of what cisgender women are perceived to be—which itself isn't a reality—and if she didn't, she wasn't considered to be "real." The same restrictions applied for transgender men. This repressive rule was illustrated for me one night at a convenience store right off Thirteenth Street.

Jay, a transgender man, and Denise, a transgender woman, collided in the candy aisle. The two had some evil history and constantly bickered, so running into each other at the convenience store on a steamy summer night was not great timing. Denise was well over six feet tall, with a large frame and epic breasts. She was often harassed and known to carry weapons in a huge, pink leather purse: mace and a massive blade. Denise did not fit the seemingly unreachable standards of cisgender femininity, but she refused to live in secrecy. She'd walk the Philadelphia streets in broad daylight, unapologetic and proud. When transphobes on the streets threatened her, she'd whip out her blade and prepare to slice. Many straight boys who bullied Denise thought they were about to meet their maker when that blade popped out of her pink purse. Denise would chase them for half a block; eventually she'd let them go, adjust her twenty-two-inch mane, and continue on her way.

Jay was short, no more than eighteen, drowning in baggy clothes. He walked with a slight pimp stroll and always maintained a hard look on his face. As a transgender man, he appeared to still be searching to find comfort in his identity. Jay was extremely aggressive, and when he saw Denise in the candy aisle, his mouth started running. "Damn, bitch! You looking rough today—like a retired football player!" Laughter erupted in the convenience store, and I kept my eye on that pink purse.

"Jay," Denise began, "I'm telling you, I'm not in the mood right now."

"I bet you that pussy smell like Old Spice!" Jay hollered.

"Jay, I'm not feeling it tonight," Denise warned.

"I'm sorry—you don't have no pussy!" Jay spat, grabbing his crotch. Denise walked past Jay dismissively, heading to the cashier. Onlookers cackled as Jay followed her, stopping by a pyramid of Snapple bottles, just a few feet away from Denise. "Yep, no pussy. You got a shriveled dick between your legs!" Denise dropped her purse, tossed her hair over her shoulder, pulled her arm back, and, with what looked like all the force she could muster, hit Jay with an uppercut directly on his jaw. The sound of Denise's fist making contact with Jay's jaw echoed through the store as he collapsed into the Snapple bottles, causing the pyramid to crash. The cashier screamed, and the "kids" in the convenience store cheered for the drama. Denise yelled at Jay, "You wanna feel like a man, bitch? Well, I'll beat your ass like a man!" While Jay cried in the Snapple mess, Denise fixed her hair, grabbed her purse, and pumped out of the store. I was grateful the blade never made an appearance.

Even in the freedom of Thirteenth Street, the constructs of gender set unreasonable demands. Deidra was beloved for presenting as a "real" woman, managing to grab a bit more privilege from her own community. However, Denise battled abuse both from outside and from within her community. Jay struggled with the trauma of toxic masculinity. We were all victims, regardless of alleged safe spaces. Thirteenth Street after hours was the closest space to escapism we could find, but the work of freedom and identity was monstrous, and the journey to practice inclusiveness from within proved to be epic.

The work was constant, especially when our escapism was tainted. Only a few blocks away sat a grimy hetero club named Fever. Many times, the straight boys wanted to flex their heterosexuality and harass people on Thirteenth Street. This never ended well. What the straight boys failed to realize was the black and Latin LGBT folks on Thirteenth Street were from the 'hood, just like them. Sexual orientation does not change your roots. Some of the straights had to learn: Never fuck with a gay hoodlum.

One particular July evening, three young men popped up on Thirteenth and Walnut Streets, overdressed in the baggy clothes of the 1990s, clearly high and feeling frisky. The strip was packed; Nikki and I were planted directly across the street from the straight boys, who were laughing and pointing at passersby.

"What are they doing?" I asked.

"Fucking with the wrong ones. The trade sometimes tries it." *Trade* was a term used to describe straight men. "But they don't know we aren't the white gay boys." Nikki's comment shook me. Clearly, homophobic attacks occur in every racial demographic of the LGBT community, but the connections between poverty, race, class, and sexual orientation are often overlooked, especially by heterosexuals who think of gay black men as weak. Gay black men are dealt the blows of unachievable standards of manhood. Therefore, the double consciousness of blackness and gayness often manifests into rage, especially when pushed by antagonizers who believe you are a sissy, punk, or faggot.

A tall, heavyset young man wearing a backwards baseball cap, whom I recognized from the strip but didn't know personally, was walking toward the straight men with his arm around his boyfriend, who was just as big. Believing they were within the safety of Thirteenth Street, their guard was down; they didn't foresee the ignorance ahead until they arrived at the corner with the straight men, one of whom let out a holler. "Yo! These two big niggas is faggots? What the fuck? Y'all look like you should be fighting, not fucking!"

In the bombastic energy of Thirteenth Street, I heard a rare hush go over the strip. The sound of blatant bigotry traveled; heads turned and stared. We were all triggered. These boys thought we were animals in the zoo. They came onto our territory to terrorize. The one space we owned, even if it was just for a few hours after midnight, was being infiltrated by the very people we were attempting to escape. These men represented our fathers, grandfathers, brothers, and high school bullies. "I hope he fucks them up," Nikki said.

"Nigga, you got a fucking problem?" the tall man raged, pulling away from his boyfriend and charging right up to the biggest of the three straight boys. Like sharks, the crowd on Thirteenth Street circled around them. The straight boy clearly felt threatened and made the unwise decision to flex his so-called masculinity.

"Fuck you, fag—" Before he could finish, a wrecking ball of a fist rammed directly into his forehead, stunning him as he toppled to the ground. Eyes huge, he looked up at the man who knocked him on his ass. One of the other boys whipped out a blade, and the third boy appeared to grab for another weapon in his pocket, which was when Nikki and I instantly jumped at least fifty feet back. Like superheroes, and before anyone could see what the second weapon was, a crowd of gay boys, trans women, trans men, lesbians, loyal straight girls, and others who could not be put in a box started a mini-riot on Thirteenth and Walnut Streets. The three boys disappeared into a storm of punches, kicks, and swinging purses and backpacks, beating the trade into the steamy Philadelphia cement.

The wild beating went on for several minutes until sirens blared. "Maggie is on her way!" someone yelled as the band of LGBT rebels vanished in seconds, leaving the straight boys battered, rolling around shirtless on the concrete. The tall man was the only one still standing there, glaring at them. "Keep your dumb asses off Thirteenth Street, bitches," he threatened. "Don't think because I'm gay that I won't fuck you up." The cops were coming closer. Straight or LGBT, no black person wanted to be caught after a fight and shirtless by the Philadelphia police.

"We gotta get out of here," one of the boys mumbled. They sloppily gathered themselves, running and limping down Walnut Street. They never returned to Thirteenth Street after midnight.

"I love Thirteenth Street," I said to Nikki, who giggled. "Where else am I going to see straight men get their asses beat by every damn person in the community?" I don't condone violence, and it's important to remember we were angst-ridden teenagers or in our complicated early twenties. That said, the demand for respect that day affirmed my blackness and my gayness. I was bullied all my life and told never to fight back, to "just ignore it." If you did fight back, you'd never win against the bullies, but we were all willing to fight to protect our safe space. Thirteenth Street and its lovable, crazy personalities represented the freedom of youth, which was rare for young black LGBT people in Philadelphia at the time. Here, the tables didn't just turn, they spun on society's axis.

Another safe space on Thirteenth Street was a nightclub called the Nile, which sat on the corner of Thirteenth and Locust Streets. I had been hearing about the Nile from Nikki for months and expected a glamorous venue with multiple floors and dancers in exotic costumes—wrong. You would never have known it was a club, with its decaying brown wooden door that seemed to be camouflaged into the aged building. If it weren't for the burly security guard standing outside, I wouldn't have seen the entrance.

"This is it?" I asked as the guard let us in.

"Yeah, child," Nikki answered, like I was being ungrateful. The music blasted from upstairs as I paid cash beneath a thick plastic window to a thin, older woman with a cigarette in her mouth and a bright smile.

"This is his first time here!" Nikki yelled joyfully.

The woman looked at me, dramatically pulled the cigarette from her mouth, and said, "Well, get your goddamn life!"

"Yes, bitch!" Nikki screamed, tossing her the cash as she grabbed my hand, excitedly running up a flight of stairs with the music becoming louder. "I need a beat, honey!"

There were no multiple floors or exotic dancers, but the Nile didn't need the glamour; there was magic in that unmarked building. An ancient disco ball twirled above a black-and-white checkered floor and a massive deejay booth orchestrated powerful, tribal music. The dark lights of the club silhouetted people running back and forth across the dance floor, possessed by the rhythms. The movements were unlike anything I had ever seen. Legs kicking, arms swinging, heads spinning, and bodies stretching. Black and brown people of various genders and expressions were African dancing in this LGBT club. African dance revolved around praising ancestors, but out of the several times I witnessed African dance, this was the first time I felt people were actually *praising*.

On the other side of the club, I saw an extremely different style of dancing. Boys and girls swung their arms gracefully, jumped into the air, and slammed to the floor, but their movements were perfectly suited to the hard house beats. People surrounded them, hollering out things that were barely audible against the loud music.

"What's that dance they're doing?" I yelled to Nikki over the music, pointing to the crowd that surrounded two people.

"That's voguing. Oh! They're battling!"

Nikki ran toward the circle, and I followed, not wanting to stand by myself. The two young men tossed their arms as if they were boneless, creating movements I had only seen in Mortal Kombat. Voguing resembled breakdancing, but it was extremely feminine in the most liberating way. Their faces were confident, nearly arrogant, with each move pushing the crowd deeper into a frenzy.

"This is so cool," I screamed in Nikki's ear, but she was cheering with everyone else. After minutes of battling and soaked in sweat, one of the young men stopped voguing, clearly exhausted. They gave each other a quick hug as the crowd broke up into their own versions of voguing. I was about to ask Nikki if she could vogue when I heard a long, operatic scream come from the back of the club, near a tiny stage. Nikki grabbed my hand and pulled me through the crowd, running toward the continuous scream. We reached the mini-stage, where we saw a tall, lean, older, beautifully dark man in a bedazzled hot-red thong and a purple cape that flowed down his back. He whipped his hips back and forth, swung his hands from side to side, spun in three circles with the cape flying in the Nile wind, and roared, "Get your life, children!" before letting out another operatic scream.

Nikki joined in on the scream, mouth wide, flinging her arms as high as possible and affirming with a wail, "Yes, bitch!" I shook Nikki, trying to get her attention. I needed to know who this person was.

"Who's that?" I yelled about four times.

Breaking Nikki out of her Nile trance, she stopped, placed both her hands on her hips, and said, "That's the mothafuckin' Phantom! He *is* the dance floor!" The Phantom leaped from the stage, screamed wildly, and shimmied from one side of the dance floor to the other. He gripped a speaker with both hands and let out another shimmy, fell up against the wall to shimmy again—almost like a preacher in the church who laid hands on his congregation, the Phantom shot around the dance floor, seeking out his next shimmy location.

I was dumbfounded, circling to keep my eyes on the Phantom. I needed to see more of him. His soul was huge, and every person in the club encouraged him with church-like shouting. Then the Phantom spotted me, frozen on the dance floor. He locked eyes with me and appeared to fly over, his purple cape in full flight. Jiggling in the red thong, the Phantom placed his hands on my shoulders and bellowed with eyes wide and mouth huge, "Bitch! You betta turn this mothafucka out!"

Overwhelmed in the best way, I rested against a random wall, letting myself be absorbed by the feelings of liberation that overcame me. The Nile dismantled my previous so-called normal world. I found an atmosphere where everyone appeared secure in their nuanced identities, which was exactly what I was searching for. The souls in the Nile were not concerned with mythological limitations. The Nile was the personification of freedom.

Immersed in Thirteenth Street and the Nile, I began dating, and by August I landed a semi-boyfriend. I was eighteen years old, dating a twenty-four-year-old who was jealous, intense, and dramatic. Young and beyond dumb, I couldn't see the obvious signs. Nikki warned me about him and repeatedly said, "The faggotry is gonna bust out of him soon. My titties can feel it."

One evening, I told my boyfriend that Nikki and I were headed to the Nile. He started huffing and puffing, questioning why I ran the streets while I was in a relationship. Again, I was eighteen, and we had been dating for no more than three weeks. I met up with Nikki, proudly ignoring his foolishness. By around two a.m., Nikki and I were getting every fiber of our life on the dance floor when my boyfriend stormed into the club, barreling toward us. "Now, bitch," Nikki said with a deep sigh. In my eighteen-year-old mind, I knew the relationship was almost over. Nonetheless, we said our hellos and I quickly jumped back onto the dance floor with Nikki. After an hour, just when I was about to forget that my boyfriend was in the building, he grabbed my arm and violently pulled me to the back of the club. "I gotta talk with you!" he demanded.

"What the hell do you want?" I snapped. "You're getting on my nerves!"

"Those two boys over there are about to jump Nikki!" He pointed to two young men who were known for fighting.

"Why would they want to jump Nikki?"

"I don't know, but I heard them say, 'Get her!' We should leave, because they looked serious!"

I pulled Nikki off the dance floor and explained what my boyfriend had said. She was just as confused. "Why would those butch queens want to jump me? I'm a fuckin' lady!" I didn't have an answer to Nikki's question, and although I knew my boyfriend was crazy, I didn't believe he would create such an elaborate lie.

My boyfriend shouted, "We have to go! I don't want anything to happen to either of you! Let's go now!" Nikki and I were still unsure, but in fear and knowing that my boyfriend knew more people than we did, we agreed to leave. As we walked to the train, he kept up the drama, recounting all the beatings he had seen over the years. "I remember when they broke someone's leg! I remember when they cut someone in the face! I remember when they were on the news for assault!" *Nikki and I may have dodged a serious beatdown,* I thought.

The next morning, afternoon, and evening, Nikki complained incessantly. "Where am I going to go to get my life? Where I am going to go to get a go-go?" She was completely distressed over losing her outlet. The Nile wasn't just a club; it was a place of worship. This had been Nikki's space for freedom for three years, and it had also become my freedom space. The Nile was the sole black and Latin LGBT nightclub in Philadelphia, the only house club. This was the one space where we could be ourselves, which is crucial for young people. Now we were told there was a mark on Nikki's head and we shouldn't attend. Nikki was delirious. We ended up at my boyfriend's house, demanding more details. It was a Saturday night and we needed to feel a beat.

My boyfriend insisted that the two boys were about to drag Nikki out and bash her. He told the story again and stressed we'd be the biggest fools in Philly to return to the Nile. "Isn't your safety more important than house music?" my boyfriend pleaded. I thought for a minute, looking to Nikki for an answer.

"Child, please," she said dismissively. "I'm going to be safe. I just need some protection."

"What kind of protection?" I asked.

"I'm going to the Nile tonight. I'm not gonna be afraid to walk in a damn club. I'm from North Philly!" Nikki declared. "So, I'll go to the club and see what happens, but if I do get knocked, I need something to defend myself with. Where are your knives?" Nikki asked my boyfriend.

"What are you going to do with a knife?" I questioned, not sure of her plan. Nikki rummaged through my boyfriend's silverware and found a long, sharp steak knife. "How are you going to bring a knife into the club? The security guards will find it!" I warned, seriously confused.

"Not with these big titties, doll." Nikki parted her huge breasts and slid the knife right into her cleavage, and like magic, the blade disappeared. Nikki adjusted herself, checked that her bra was secure, and said, "If someone tries to knock me—I'll cut a bitch! Mama always told me these big breasts would come in handy!"

"This is the dumbest shit I have ever seen," my boyfriend complained, clearly giving up. "Go to the club at your own risk."

Nikki danced the night away, revolving every movement around her breasts. She shook, caressed, and struck poses with her bosom, all with her eye on the two evil boys in the club. Nikki was popular, and every person who said a hello put her on edge, but she was ready to slay—literally.

In the end, Nikki never got jumped, and the people who my boyfriend claimed wanted to attack her said hello with no malice. Nikki and I always believed that my boyfriend made up the story to get me out of the club. Less than a week later, he and I were no more. Sometimes I wish someone tried to attack Nikki that night. It would have been a story of legend: "Someone tried to knock Nikki and she pulled a blade out of her titties like She-Ra!"

In those days, I wasn't much of a dancer; I mainly came to Thirteenth Street and the Nile to be with my tribe. After making sure there would be no beatdown, Nikki grabbed my hand, forcing me onto the dance floor.

"This is my favorite! Listen to the words of this song!" she said, shaking her breasts with the blade still in place.

The song that wailed through the club caught my ear, repeating the three words, "I've been blessed!" I moved, letting the music consume me. A tear crept from my eye. I was getting salvation. I was eighteen, and I found my people. No matter how complicated or messy, this was my tribe. My heart knew that my time on Thirteenth Street and in the Nile was a seminal moment in my journey. I often questioned blessings, but the words to "I've Been Blessed" acknowledged me. Regardless of what anyone in the world thought or believed, I was blessed.

ASKING FOR IT

4

THE CLUB WAS THICK WITH PEOPLE. THERE WAS NOWHERE to catch my breath. The music wailed like a subway train, pounding through my skull with manic and intoxicating beats. "You all right?" someone asked, sounding concerned, but I wasn't sure if it was shade. I was high as the universe, vacillating between a nightmare and an equally horrific reality.

"Yeah, child," I spat. Eyes examined my entire body. I turned away. I was in shambles. My mind wasn't sure what was real. The person in front of me had no gender or color, their voice unrecognizable.

"A few months ago you were the prettiest boy in Philly," the person said. "Why are you letting that man do this to you?"

"Bitch, please!" I pushed the person out of the way and headed to the dance floor, where the deejay was mixing a nasty version of "Cuban Pete." I was getting higher on the rhythms when I felt a tap on my shoulder. Stumbling, I turned around to lock eyes with my boyfriend, Omar. He was twenty years older than me, we were living together, and he dealt drugs. Quite the trite story, dating an older drug dealer, but he was my first love. We grinded on the dance floor. He was a dream come true for many of the boys in the club: masculine, muscular, and money.

"I need you to do something for me," he yelled over the music. He gently took my hand, guiding me to the back of the club. This was where everyone sneaked to share their weed, coke, pills, and other vices. He pulled me into the bathroom, squeezing our way toward the last stall.

"Why are we here?" I asked, scoping out the grime. The mirrorless bathroom was packed, mostly an older crowd, filling the small room with pungent odors of marijuana, cigarette smoke, alcohol, and other smells that I forced myself to ignore. The walls were stained with frantic writing. The faces were drugged-out zombies, giving Omar a heavy-eyed hello. He pulled out a straw, made a white line on his forearm, and told me to take the hit. Just like he taught me, I placed the straw to my nose and snorted.

"I need you to do something for me," he casually said again, handing me a bottle of Hennessy. I took a quick gulp.

"We have to do it in here?" I asked, swallowing more Hennessy, trying to take my mind away from the grotesque bathroom. As I felt the flawless high in my head, he pushed me up against the stall with the door closed.

"One of my clients is in there," he explained, softly tapping on the door. "I fucked up again. Didn't pay him the right amount for everything he supplied me with....You helped me use those drugs." I stood with my back against the stall as Omar hovered over me like a giant. Dizziness wracked my brain; I gazed around the bathroom trying to make out a familiar face through the dark clouds of smoke.

"What do you want me to do?" I asked.

"Just go in there and suck his dick till he says stop. He told me he'd forget about the money if you do it. He likes you."

"Huh?" I said, not sure what he was asking. Suck some man's dick? For money? "No, Omar. I gotta go." I pushed him away with the little strength I had in my drugged body. Like tentacles, his large hand with rough calluses wrapped around my neck, squeezing my throat slightly. Omar's eyes were huge, dilated. I knew he was on every pill and snort possible. A slow terror sunk into my heart, but I wasn't quick enough to fight.

"Haven't I done a lot for you? You need somewhere to live, don't you? You need to eat, don't you? You want to get high, don't you? Everybody's got to pay. I never ask you for shit. You're asking for it." His features were different, sharper than before, almost animated. I recognized him but didn't know him. Sweat beads popped over his bald head, a sign of anger. "I'll be right outside the door. Just fucking do it." I didn't move. Omar squeezed harder on my throat, cutting off my air. He kissed my cheek and carefully opened the stall door. I prayed the creaking of the door would wake me from my nightmare, but everything felt too real. I pleaded with my eyes, searching for something humane in him. I stepped a few inches into the stall until

I bumped into something. Omar nodded, released my neck, "Just do it. I'll be right here." I heard his body lean up against the door, so I couldn't escape.

A house remix of "And I Am Telling You" by Jennifer Holliday blared. My mind was in a deep fog, my throat dry. I was trapped. I couldn't run. I couldn't fight. I was in a nightmare. I turned around and faced a short, fat white man with crooked glasses and a dirty gray business suit. His slacks were around his ankles. His man breasts pushed against his tight suit. He stroked a tiny, plump, pink dick that emerged from his reddish, flabby, hairy thighs. He salivated at the sight of me, like a slave master waiting to be serviced. I recognized him. He was one of a handful of white men in the club who had a fetish for black boys. He supplied drugs and paid cheap rates to fuck and get sucked by the boys who were marginalized and trapped. There were no worries of anyone fighting back.

"Hey, boy, suck my cock." His tongue hung out of thin lips. What if he had a knife or a gun? No one ever said no to him. How would I escape? This entrapment was a metaphor for all of the doors that were closed. No bootstraps to pull myself up by. I was not valuable. I'd be another dead black boy at a gay club in Philly and no one would care, not even Omar. There was already a graveyard of black gay men who were being killed off by HIV, poverty, homelessness, drugs, and predators. I lowered my head and let the tears drop; I wanted everything to be over. I fell down to my knees, feeling the wetness on the tiled floor. The beast put his slimy hands on the back of my head. "Suck my cock, boy," he ordered again, relishing my distress.

The beast wasn't circumcised; I smelled the stench of cheese. Nothing can last forever, this is a nightmare. I had to live through this to make it out on the other side. I put my mouth on his dick and sucked my soul away. He moaned, sweated, and snorted like a barbarian. I saw violet. My tears dripped on his fat legs. I begged for it to be over, begged for it to stop. Begged for someone to save me from the gutter. I was gutless. The minutes dragged as the beast grunted. The smell of weed, shit, piss, alcohol, dick, and a dying boy nearly made me vomit. I was going to vomit on the beast's dick, and he might kill me. He snorted and moaned. I felt his poison hit the inside of my mouth. He pushed my head back, making me hit the door; I was almost awake. His toxic white ooze dripped, creating more stains on the floor. I spit out his mess, choking as I banged on the stall. Omar slowly opened the door and looked at the slovenly beast, knowing I had done his bidding.

"Good boy," he said with a smile. I shoved my way to the bathroom sink,

causing the zombies to groan. With the little water that came out of the fau-
cet, I washed my mouth and face. This was a bottom I never knew existed.
Omar came up behind me, and I felt his hard dick through his clothes. I
turned around so he could see the mess he'd made. He gave me the straw. To
escape, to run away, to find that cloud that would take me higher than this
planet, I took another hit. I heard "I'm sorry" at some point during the next
few hours, but there was no need to respond.

This was my nightmare.

"A few months ago you were the prettiest boy in Philly. Why are you letting that man do this to you?" I asked Jacob. I barely knew the boy, but I
saw myself in him. He was my mirror. We had a similar look, we were the
same age, and he was dating my ex. Omar was intoxicating, charming, and
from the start, he cast a vicious spell on me. I was obsessed with his voice,
his walk, and strong presence. When I found out Omar dealt and used drugs,
lied about his age, and was a disturbing control freak, I ended the relationship—mainly because my protective friends gave me no choice. I had a support system, a tribe who loved fiercely. Jacob had no one; he was "new to the
scene" and Omar's perfect victim.

"Bitch, please!" Jacob spat, pushing me away and stumbling toward the
dance floor. I saw Omar come up to him from behind. Jacob wrapped his
arms around his neck. Soon, they were walking hand in hand to the back of
the club. Curious, I followed my ex-boyfriend and his new teenage dream.
I squeezed into the crowded and disgusting bathroom to see Omar giving
Jacob drugs to snort. The exchange looked confusing and tense, and eventually Omar's hands were around Jacob's throat.

Within seconds, Jacob was in the bathroom stall while Omar leaned
against the door. I waited, not sure what was happening. When I saw Jacob
topple out of the stall, rinsing his mouth out in the sink and an older white
man following, buttoning up his slacks, I knew exactly what happened.
Omar pimped out Jacob. The grimy white man was a known face in the
club, famous for supplying drugs and paying any addict he could find to suck
his smelly dick.

A rage swept over me as I bulldozed my way out of the bathroom, charged
through the dance floor, and barreled out of the club's doors. Philadelphia's
warm nighttime air cleared out my lungs as I breathed deeply on the corner
of Thirteenth and Locust Streets. It was somewhere around three a.m. A

random car slowly drove by with Madonna's "Secret" pumping out of the speakers. The car honked as I turned away, walking quickly down the street.

I saw myself in Jacob. I was one bad decision away from being him. One support system away from Omar's hands around my throat. One mistake away from being under a deadly influence. I sensed every piece of my heart in Jacob, and it haunted me. I was "out of the closet," but I wasn't free from predators. I functioned in an environment that remained vigilant in its attempts to destroy me. There was no grand reward for being authentic. My soul was up for grabs. There was no magic in my sexuality. I found my tribe, but I still existed in identities that were not valued.

HOW SEX WORKERS
TAUGHT ME
5 TO HUSTLE

SUMMER, 1995. FRIDAY AND *SPECIES* WERE BLOWING UP AT the box office. Groove Theory's "Tell Me" and Notorious B.I.G.'s "One More Chance (Remix)" were in heavy rotation on my Sony Walkman. I had just graduated from high school in Philadelphia, and despite having struggled with what felt like unreachable standards of black masculinity since childhood, my challenges with my sexual orientation nearly vanished when I felt the lips of another guy for the first time. There was no great debate in my soul. The natural emotion I felt from a man was something I never felt with a woman. Also, I found people who loved me and provided a space for conversation and freedom. I wasn't alone.

My friends and I were fixtures on Thirteenth Street. Before the City of Brotherly Love was gentrified, the strip was known as "Freak Street," especially after midnight, when most of the white gays headed home and the black and Latin LGBT kids held court. We were street urchins who terrified the white gay community and black heterosexuals. We didn't believe in same-sex marriage; we were anti-marriage. We proudly called ourselves dykes, trannies, fags, queens, butches, and drags—all unacceptable language by today's standards. The intersection of class, race, and sexuality was evident in our unique slang, tribal house music, and crafty survival skills.

Like clockwork, I strolled up Thirteenth Street every night, trekking to the club, which didn't open until one a.m. and didn't get hot for another two hours. There was usually a group of sex workers on the corner of Sansom and Thirteenth, the majority of whom were black and Latin trans women.

Initially, I was terrified by these women. I had no experience with them; they had been torn down by a mid-1990s economy, never allowed in the workforce, and education was inaccessible to them due to rampant discrimination. Because of my own internalized prejudices, their exterior shook my soul.

For weeks, I hurried past their gaze as I dashed up Thirteenth Street. These were the same women I would see in the club later that night, but in my stupid mind, I feared being associated with them. They could feel my disdain for them.

However, one particular woman was deeply insulted that I wouldn't speak to her when we crossed paths. "Hey, faggot!" she screamed after we locked eyes and I turned away. Attempting to channel a "Freak Like Me"-era Adina Howard in red leather hot pants, a black corset, and a short hairdo, she spat, "I see your ass down here every weekend, bitch—you ain't gonna speak?"

"I don't know you!" I shot back, startling myself.

"Mothafucka, I know *you* and you ain't that cute!" she sassed as I sped up. "Didn't your mama teach you to speak to people when you see them? I'm a damn human being!"

"These young faggots..." I heard another woman mumble in a tone that was more disappointed than angry.

The next night, Adina spotted me from a distance walking up the other side of Thirteenth Street. I couldn't believe she could see me from so far away. "There he go!" she hollered. I moved quickly, but she stomped across the street, necklaces, bracelets, and earrings jingling in unison. Adina stood before me, blocking my escape. I was scared for my life.

"You are gonna *see* me," she demanded in a surprisingly calm voice.

It was at that point something in my teenage brain clicked. I had not truly seen her before that moment. It occurred to me that I had often walked by her like she was garbage on the corner, the same way angry heterosexuals leered at my friends and me if they accidentally wandered down Thirteenth Street after midnight. Although I was never a sex worker, Adina and I were both part of the black and Latin LGBT community, living on the fringes of society.

"I'm sorry," I mumbled, eyes down as I squeezed my hands together in terror.

"You are sorry! You're sorry and you're tired!" Adina shouted. "Now, next time you walk down this goddamn street, you make sure you show some respect and speak to us. Got it?" I nodded my head. "Go on now to that club."

From that moment on, I made it a point to *see* Adina.

Every night I walked down the street, I gave a hello to Adina and her friends. Eventually, I walked down their side of the street and stopped to talk. She illuminated so much for a young, impressionable teenager, and in her own brilliant way, she taught me life skills. She could clock someone's story with one glance: "He's gonna wanna get fucked," "He's gonna be cheap," or "He's gonna be a rough client." More often than not, she was right.

"How are you able to figure someone out so quickly?" I asked her.

She smiled. "All you have to do is ask one question," she explained. "As long as you nod your head and look like you fucking care, they'll tell you their life story." As frightful as she originally appeared to me, Adina owned that superpower and could flip the switch, making anyone she chose feel instantly comfortable. I studied how she spoke to strangers, from lost tourists and drive-by homophobes to potential tricks.

There were other lessons, too. The type no school will ever teach.

People have asked me if it is hard to debate on live television. In many ways, it's not hard at all—I learned from the streets and sex workers like Adina. Though I wasn't a constant fixture on the corner with the ladies of the night, whenever I passed by I always made it a point to stop and say hello. Several times, I would catch them in fiery debates about politics, pop culture, and fashion, talking hot topics years before *The View* arrived on morning television. They were plugged into the world unlike anyone I knew.

"Bill Clinton is a fucking joke, girl!" I remember one argument beginning. "Y'all dumb bitches think because he played a damn saxophone, he's for you? He kicked women off welfare! He's locking up more niggas than ever! He is ignoring AIDS. Child, please!"

When locked in debate on television or among friends, a look of derision might wash over my face, my head slightly askew and lips pursed; it is a signature rejoinder I employ from time to time. The stare says all I need to say: *Child, please!*

Adina and her friends struggled with the daily horrors of sex work—harassment from the police, violent clients, and passersby. Unlike drug dealers, transgender sex workers are a subculture within a subculture that has never been glorified. The stereotypical dealer is sometimes valorized as sexy, masculine, and "doing what he's gotta do" to survive. Trans sex workers, especially the percentage that are trans women of color, are considered by some to be disease-infested night predators, abominations. Once, I remember stupidly asking Adina, "Why are you out here? You're so smart. Do you really want to do this for the rest of your life?"

"You think I *want* to do this?" she snapped, reminding me of our first encounter. Noticing my apologetic look, she softened. "Look at me, Clay," she replied, opening her arms and averting her eyes downward. "No one is going to hire *me*. Someone is gonna hire you. You got it made and you don't even know it." Adina didn't fit the often unattainable standards of cisgender norms, nor did she have access to proper health care, education, career opportunities, or even protection from the law. She was constantly pushed deeper into a structure of exploitation.

"Some dreams don't come true," she said as a black Jeep Cherokee honked directly across the street. A white man rolled down his window, motioning for Adina to come over to him. The man in the Jeep looked near insane, with a bald head and more piercings than I could count. He cut me a look with his bloodshot eyes, giving me chills. Adina coyly held up a finger to indicate she'd be right there. She adjusted her breasts and turned to me, "How do I look?"

"You couldn't look any better," I replied, soaking in her sadness. We smiled at each other, but what hung in the air, for me, was a feeling of resignation.

"I need to live," she stressed. "It's fast money, baby." With a wink, Adina strutted across the street, hopping into the Jeep and giving the man a quick kiss on the lips. She gave me a dainty wave. I heard the snap of the automatic locks as the tinted windows rolled up. They drove off, speeding down Thirteenth Street.

I moved to New York City a few years later, and over the course of a decade, my writing career kicked off. I was interviewing celebrities, writing editorials, but not getting paid a dime. I did the work to build my credentials as a writer. I'd walk into a room using the skills I learned from Adina; no matter the celebrity or politician, I was now a master at figuring someone out in seconds.

I vividly remember the first time I was paid for an assignment. I earned $150 for a twenty-minute interview with Terrence Howard. *"That's fast money!"* I thought. In that moment, I knew my walk, as a journalist, would have been vastly different without the jewels I received from Adina and the women who orbited the world of Thirteenth Street. They were witty and knowledgeable, and they selflessly understood people more than people understood them.

I am a bit more polished now. Not many would think once upon a time I was "one of the children." Based on the choices I've made, my life could've unraveled in an opposite fashion. I was fortunate enough to transition out of the neighborhood, but for many, escaping wasn't an option. The HIV/AIDS epidemic ravaged my era of Thirteenth Street kids. We were black, Latin, poor, and LGBT, which meant we were invisible. But I will never forget what I learned the summer of 1995. Adina's demand to be seen, her unique life lessons, and her unknowing encouragement uplifted me more than she could have imagined. Fortunately, the dominant narrative of trans women as sex workers is shifting. But it is important to honor these nameless, faceless women—before, now, and always.

The last time I saw Adina was in 1998. It was right before I moved to New York City. Philly was starting to gentrify, and all of my old haunts were now closed. Freak Street was on the verge of becoming another Fifth Avenue. It was the middle of the afternoon, and I spotted Adina applying for a job at a fast food restaurant. Divested of her signature nighttime attire, it took me a moment to recognize her—hair in a bun, big sunglasses, clothes lacking vibrant color—considering I'd never seen her in the daylight. In my excitement I rushed over to say hello, curious of her whereabouts. Months had passed since we had last seen each other. Without looking up, she uttered, "Clay, all I wanna do is be real. All I wanna do is walk down the street. All I wanna do is get a job, pay my taxes, and have a place to live." She sighed, eyes still hidden by the sunglasses. "How are you?" she asked softly.

"I'm good," I answered. "Moving to New York City soon."

"Live your dream, baby," she answered with a tight smile. "Let me fill out these applications." I stepped away. I knew she wanted to be alone.

"I'll see you soon," I said with a wave as she slowly nodded back. I turned away, but quickly glanced back. Adina was staring into space, not filling out the application. This was not the Adina I knew. Although her conviction for survival was there, the spark was gone. All I could think was society had claimed another victim in its war against trans women of color.

Adina passed away the next year.

SUZIE Q

BORN AND RAISED ON THE AGGRESSIVE STREETS OF NORTH Philly, Tony never lived in a closet a day of his black gay life. By the ninth grade, he proudly came out, proclaiming to anyone who would listen, "I'm gay, get over it." In the tenth grade, he landed a boyfriend. By the eleventh grade, his mother, a former drug addict who allegedly found Jesus, had thrown him out of the house. Throughout high school, Tony traveled across various couches in the City of Brotherly Love, including mine. Thursday nights were reserved for him at my tiny apartment in West Philadelphia. Only three years apart in age, Tony and I bonded; beyond just "gay brothers," he became family.

Tony was short, thin, and effeminate. Naturally stylish, he had the gift to reinvent rags into high-octane fashion. "I'm a crafty faggot!" he'd declare in the mirror as he prepared for school. He'd take a basic button-up shirt, cut off the sleeves, bleach the front, add some beads and trinkets—and magically transform the garment into mid-nineties urban glamour.

By the time Tony graduated from high school, he was authentic wherever he stood. He refused to limit his flair to Thirteenth Street. He could not be tamed. His mouth could set anyone on fire. He never feared an argument or throwing hands. One afternoon, the freedom of Thirteenth Street came with us to downtown Philadelphia. We had driven to the shopping district to make a run to Banana Republic. Tony wanted to lay his eyes on "the overpriced clothes white people pay for." As we were getting out of Tony's barely drivable car, he was laughing loudly at a random joke I'd made, throwing his hands in the air and mocking that he was clutching pearls.

He locked his car door and came over to the other side of the car, where I was, to lock the passenger door. The door could only lock from the outside with his key—yes, the car was on its last legs. As Tony struggled with the lock, I saw a man and a woman down the block, standing on the corner. I recognized a familiar fire in the man's eyes. A danger. He was pointing at us and shaking his head. The man stood well over six feet, muscular, in his late twenties, and clearly uncomfortable at two men not performing his idea of masculinity. He shot furtive glances, back and forth, at us.

"Tony," I said, as he closed the car door.

"This door ain't gonna lock, fuck it. Ain't nobody gonna steal this car."

"That guy on the corner. Do you know him?" Tony looked and said he had never seen the man in his life. "Well, he's tripping."

"What the fuck y'all faggots looking at?" the man roared, noticing us both staring. I knew this story. He saw "faggots" on the street and wanted to flex his manhood.

"Y'all need to stop acting like that on the street!" added the woman, who appeared to be his girlfriend.

"Y'all faggots are all over Philly!" the man yelled, making people stare.

Tony rolled his neck and belted out, "What the fuck are you gonna do about it, nigga?" The man's jaw unhinged. The woman's eyes widened like saucers as she grabbed the man's arm, trying to calm his homophobic rage.

"Why are you paying attention to us?" I loudly questioned. "We're minding our business and you're worrying about what two faggots are doing?" The man tried to pull his girlfriend off him. He was ready to brawl.

"No!" she screamed. "Don't go over there!" She held her grip on him. He was seconds from breaking away.

"It's time for Miss Suzie Q!" Tony yelled as he swung the car door open and dived into the backseat.

"Who the hell is Suzie Q?" I asked, bracing myself as the man broke away from his girlfriend and charged down the street.

Tony swiftly popped out of the car and whipped out a huge, rusted hammer that was nearly as long as his forearm. "This is mothafuckin' Suzie Q!" he bellowed, gripping the hammer in his hand like a North Philly version of Thor, pointing at the man who was only a few feet from us. The man stopped, eyes fixed on the hammer, and nearly tripped over himself. The woman screeched.

"Come on, nigga! You wanna feel it?" Tony yelled as he began stomping toward the man, who quickly spun around and dashed down the street, leaving the woman in his dust.

"You just gonna leave me here?" the woman yelled as she ran after him. Tony turned back around with the hammer in his hand, his other hand on his hip, lips pursed. I laughed from my soul.

"Tony! You have a hammer in your car?"

"Yes, I do—Suzie Q!" Tony confirmed as he opened the car door and tossed the hammer into the backseat. "I'm a small gay boy. These straight boys wanna try me and I need protection."

"Have you ever used it?" I asked.

"Nope. Seeing it is enough. I don't leave my house without Suzie Q. No lady is sure at night!"

In retrospect, what if Tony used Suzie Q? We were young, fearless, and clearly dumb. Suzie Q as a source of protection was a lie, but at the time, it was a lie we could believe, regardless of the realistic repercussions. Tony never used Suzie Q and eventually retired her from the backseat of his car.

Two years later, Tony called me after work, like usual. But this time he sounded shell-shocked. "I hate straight people. I fucking hate straight people," he mumbled before I could say hello.

"What happened?" I quizzed. Tony wasn't easily shaken up. He was resilient, a fighter who clawed his way up from the horrors of 1980s and 1990s Philadelphia. He landed a solid job at a nonprofit, was in college and living on his own. However, there isn't always a reward for beating the so-called odds. The fight never really ends, it just takes on new opponents.

Tony parked outside of his apartment building. Exhausted from work, he took a deep breath before exiting the car. There were eyes on him. He looked ahead and saw three men staring. They were leaning on the second car in front of him. Tony remembered Suzie Q. *Why did I put that bitch in retirement?* he thought. He looked in the backseat for something. There was no relative protection.

Hoping they were just ignorant straight boys, Tony avoided eye contact and quickly jumped out of the car. He heard the men laughing, which he knew was about his outfit: bright colors, tight slacks, and an ascot around his neck. "This nigga!" one of them yelled. "He look like one of Janet Jackson's dancers!" Tony ignored their cackles and rushed to his apartment building.

"Yo, faggot! You gonna ignore me, faggot?" They were getting closer. Tony was only a few feet away from the front door of his building. "A bitch like you don't even know how to speak?" Tony reached the door but fumbled with his keys. He felt a hand slam onto his shoulder. Gripping the keys in his fist, Tony blindly threw his arm back with all his force, pounding the fist into the man's chest, making him scream. Tony spun around. The guy was holding his chest, his shirt ripped, with small drops of blood starting to form. There was a little blood on the keys. Tony had broken the skin.

The man slammed Tony against the apartment building door. But Tony wasn't going down without a brutal fight. He attacked like he had so many times in elementary, middle school, and on his childhood block. He landed some punches on the first guy, but his two friends quickly joined.

The first punch bashed the side of his skull as stars flooded his sight. With a hand around his neck, he was dragged away from the door. A kick to Tony's knees made him collapse on West Philly's cracked sidewalk. They pounded his small body. His insides tightened. He tried to block the blows but they had him at every angle. Tony screamed for help. Cars drove by and neighbors he saw daily walked past. Tony's assault was invisible. After one final kick with a Timberland boot to his groin, one of the men hissed, "Fucking faggot," and spit on him.

He lay on the sidewalk. The gravel cut into the back of his neck. He could feel blood in his left eye. His fingers tingled. His stomach spasmed. His breath was gone. Clothes torn and bloody, he carefully dragged himself to his building, managing to open the front door. He crawled to his first-floor apartment and unlocked the door while on his throbbing knees. He collapsed in the bathroom, broken and bloodied. Tony garnered all of his strength to pull himself up from the floor. He took his time to slowly wash away the blood, clean the wounds with hydrogen peroxide, and wrap his sores with old clothes. He stared in the mirror. Just scrapes and blood for now, battle scars both visible and invisible. Soon he would swell up.

"I hate straight people," Tony said to me on the phone, no tears, just rage. A rage he could never express. He walked through life facing an indignant hatred that was never validated. Now, he would be terrified to walk the streets in his own neighborhood.

"Did you call the police?" I asked quietly. "Maybe you should file a report."

He snapped back with, "Do I look like Matthew Shepard to you?" He silenced me. When you're a dead gay black man, there is no rally, there is no documentary. "It's time to get Suzie Q out of retirement," he added.

Tony never left his house without Suzie Q again, but he also transformed into his own Suzie Q. Being a petite gay man was too risky for Tony; he would not be a target. He actively "butched" up. He mastered masculine drag and dedicated hours to his physique at the gym. Within a couple of years, Tony was unrecognizable. He was a muscle God. He was never seen as weak again. He didn't abandon all of his flair, but safety came before his freedom.

Suzie Q can still be found in the trunk of his car—but in this incarnation, Miss Suzie is a metal baseball bat.

BALL-SHAPED
WORLD

THE BATHROOM OF NORTH PHILADELPHIA'S YMCA ON
Board Street and Girard Avenue was overcrowded with young people preparing to participate in the Philadelphia Awards Ball of 2000. I was expected to
walk New Face of the Year, but I was terrified. I watched balls for years, but
never graced the so-called floor. Yet I wanted the experience; I desired the
feel of the ballroom light. "God, I hope they don't chop me," I repeated for
the billionth time.

"They're not going to chop you!" promised Tommy, who was helping
me get dressed.

"Child, you never know, the girls are shady," someone added.

"Shut up!" Tommy snapped and began applying another layer of makeup
to my face.

"Why do I have to wear so much makeup? I feel like a drag queen," I
complained.

"Bitch, this is about the illusion. You ain't going for all natural. You're
walking face. You gotta look like a model. You have to be flawless, and
no one is fucking flawless. Again, it's the illusion!" Tommy caked on the
"paint," as they called it, and instructed me to close my eyes. He sprayed
what felt like hairspray on every inch of my face, causing me to choke. "Don't
move!" he yelled.

"What the hell?" I hollered. "Is that hairspray?"

"Yes! It makes the paint look more natural."

"I've never heard of that."

"Well, you never heard of Prada until you met me, so shut it. Where are your shoes?" I pointed to an Aldo box.

"Aldo? You don't wear Aldo shoes for a ball!" he yelled.

"You told me black shoes!" I clapped back.

"I can't!" Tommy kicked off his shoes. "These are a size ten, but they're Prada."

"I can't fit a size ten. I'm a twelve!" I complained.

Tommy, exhausted by my babbling, said, "Now, bitch, you're walking a ball. You make everything happen. The shoes, the face, the clothes—I don't care what you have or don't have. Make it fucking happen! Now, shut the fuck up, put on the shoes, and get on the floor and sell it. Goddamn!"

I stuffed my size twelve feet into the tiny shoes. I had forgotten my belt, and unfortunately, my black slacks were too baggy. Tommy tied together several shoestrings for a belt, looped it through my belt loops, and made sure the turtleneck covered up the flaw. To ensure the turtleneck snatched my body, he used safety pins to tighten the back and forced me into a form-fitting blazer. My eyebrows weren't dark enough for the makeup, so he brushed mascara on my eyebrows. When I saw myself in the mirror, I was awestruck at what Tommy created. My face was flawless, even toned, jawline severely defined, and the clothes appeared to fit perfectly. This was a person I had never seen. I was now a ballroom illusion. "You make it happen," Tommy repeated.

The emcee was about to close the category for New Face of the Year. I stood one step away from the makeshift runway at the YMCA, wringing my hands with terrified nervousness. The Prada shoes were stopping the blood flow in my feet. The tight turtleneck to "accentuate the carta" cut off my air supply. At any moment, I was sure the safety pins would poke my back. "Love Hangover" by Diana Ross boomed, but my gay soul felt less secure than the safety pins struggling to hold my outfit together. I tried to remember the "rehearsals" for face. Look confident, conceited, and sell it, because it's "ovah!" I prayed from my core the judges wouldn't chop me. I was walking a ball for the first time, but in the moment it felt like every person who rejected me, from my father to my classmates to even myself, were in the faces of the judges. The ball represented acceptance.

Tommy whispered, "You better serve" and dramatically pushed me onto the runway. I caught my balance quickly as I heard scattered applause from the audience, helping me build strength. It was time to perform.

"Yes!" the emcee yelled. "You betta sell it!" I barely lifted the corners of my mouth, remembering to not smile too hard; licked the front row of my teeth to prove I had no visible dental flaws; and framed my face with my hands while I emoted to the judges' panel. I chanted in my mind, "Please don't chop me! Please don't chop me!" On my face, there was no trace of doubt. Ballroom culture taught me confidence when I had none, the power of illusions and of always and forever "making it happen," no matter the circumstances.

The first thought that might come to mind when hearing about the "ball-room scene" is the 1991 documentary *Paris Is Burning* by Jennie Livings-ton, which attempted to present the lives of black and Latin LGBT people involved in the New York City ballroom circuit. However, many in the ballroom community feel that *Paris Is Burning* unfairly branded them as pros-titutes, thieves, and degenerates, mere casualties of the volatile streets of New York City. Leaders in the scene strived to prove that although they are not a flawless community, they are often misrepresented by the media.

In truth, the ballroom scene encompasses family, competition, and bound-less creativity. Ball culture symbolizes a feverish vibrancy that embraces the "unacceptable" parts of the LGBT community. As LGBT culture transitions toward "family values," there are sectors of the community who will always be distanced from *Brady Bunch*-ish paradigms. Where do groundbreaking creativity, alternative gender identities, and unapologetic sexuality fit into a "gay agenda" that aspires to assimilate into a heterosexual prototype as a way of garnering equal rights?

Picture this: a transgender woman "selling sex" in a ball category. She wears a sheer, sizzling pink fishnet jumpsuit with a Rapunzel wig flowing down to her four-inch clear stiletto heels and her bosoms barely contained— a look similar to Rihanna or vintage Madonna. Although beautiful in her own right, this amazing sight is not what many LGBT folks deem to be "appropriate" representation; they refuse to acknowledge the full spectrum of LGBT lives. As LGBT people sink into the melting pot of heterosexual America, vital areas of our community that represented non-conformity dis-solve in the political, anti-sexual, and anti-expression mix.

"Walking into a ball, you feel like everything is right. Everything that society, gay and straight, says 'no' to is 'yes' here. I remember my first ball, I felt like, wow, this is where I need to be!" says Antar Bush, a former ballroom participant who graced floor for nearly a decade. "Every gay stereotype there is, the ballroom scene embraces, no judgments—it's truly magical."

Walking balls was about the magic and the illusions, but little did I know the ability to create magic would be a talent I would need in my future career. Balls didn't teach me about fashion or dance, but, again, about always making it happen. In May of 2012, I was scheduled to interview Tony winner Audra McDonald about her performance in *Porgy and Bess* on Broadway. I was expected to be on camera, but there was no budget for makeup. Normally, I would do my own makeup at home, after learning you can't trust in-house makeup artists to properly "paint" brown skin, but it was a sizzling 90 degrees in New York City. I would sweat the makeup off in minutes. I thought back to my ballroom roots and remembered the mantra, "Make it the fuck happen."

I trekked down to the Broadway district of Manhattan, carrying a change of clothes, high-definition makeup, and other accessories. Down the street from the theater, I found a fast food restaurant, sneaked into the pungent bathroom, and set up shop in a tiny stall. Using stretching techniques I didn't know I had, I changed my clothes, applied makeup, and gave myself a shape-up with battery-operated clippers, all while chatting on a last-minute conference call. I arrived ten minutes early for the interview, and the publicist said, "You look great!" Again, make it happen. The ballroom scene taught me the lesson of the grind.

Once you make it happen, you must perform, and whenever I've doubted myself, I channeled those ballroom roots. I appeared on *The O'Reilly Factor* on Fox News in June of 2015. Jesse Watters was the cohost, and I was joined by a black conservative, Jason Riley. Before the camera started rolling, Watters was all smiles, thanking me for showing up and cracking a few jokes. Once the red light turned on, he went for my neck like we were on the ballroom floor. He threw his first question at me: "How does white supremacy create out-of-wedlock births in the black community?" I laughed. Jesse was clearly aiming for a gotcha moment. I remembered my ballroom training: always appear "unbothered."

I laid into Watters and Riley, quoting statistics and dismissing their bigoted foolishness, and before they could end the segment, I snatched more airtime than the host. When the red light went black, Jesse's television veneer dropped, and he said to me, "Wow! That was great!" I thought he would be angry, but he appreciated the "performance." I thanked him for his time and understood his on-camera shade was nothing personal.

As I walked into the green room, I said aloud, "That was like a ball." Someone asked what a ball was, and I replied, "The best media training you could ever have."

Nearly twenty years after the release of *Paris Is Burning,* and through every transition of politics in the LGBT community, the ballroom scene is still pumping, bigger and stronger than ever. Balls are held in Illinois, Kentucky, North Carolina, Georgia, France, China, and beyond. The ballroom scene can be found in nearly every corner of the world. Over four decades ago, the pioneers of ballroom culture could not have predicted these underground galas would become a coast-to-coast phenomenon. The ballroom scene managed not only to survive, but to quite successfully evolve into a thriving culture.

One factor which helps to explain the advancement of the scene is the lure. What pulls a person to participate has changed somewhat since the days of *Paris Is Burning.* Regardless of myths that racism and homophobia have nearly vanished since the 1980s and 1990s, balls provide a safe space. Transgender women are still murdered at alarming rates, and the suicide rate for youth is four times higher for those who are LGBT. There are anti-LGBT laws popping up all over the country. We are not post-homophobia. People are battling for acceptance and reconciliation for their multiple identities, and, though complicated, the ballroom community is the heart of acceptance.

For those who remain in the ballroom scene there is a huge stigma, not just from the heterosexual community, but from others in the gay community. Glenn Scott, who entered the scene in 1991, stressed, "As far as gay people who are not into the ballroom scene, it's like we are ostracized. They don't know anything about it, they think you are trash, you steal—they've got a negative connotation from things they may have heard and maybe some people have done, but they think everybody's like that." Damon Humes, a club artist and ballroom figure for over two decades, added, "Ball people are viewed as the lowest group within gay communities. If you go to clubs you're looked at in a bad way, but if you go to balls you're looked at as a faggot."

Regardless of the perception by other communities, the ballroom scene moves unapologetically forward, gaining respect and fame. Reality star

Milan Christopher, dancer Leiomy Maldonado, and model turned actress Amiyah Scott are just a few who have roots in the ballroom scene. With more popularity and outlets for the ballroom scene, the question is: Will this subculture ever become mainstream? Antar answers: "Mainstream? No! People don't really know what that word *mainstream* means. Do we really want this thing to go mainstream? When you get more mainstream it will have to be changed and tweaked—balls will have to start on time! People will have to sit in their chair to watch a category!" Glenn Scott added, "If we're not involved directly, we'll still be outcasts with something we created, which happens with everything. Gay people always create something and somehow don't get the credit for it."

No one can predict how the ballroom scene will evolve over the years to come. Regardless of the political climate, or the selective LGBT agenda, it is obvious this scene will not be ignored. Harold Balenciaga, who has been walking balls since 1996, pondered the future: "Maybe the ballroom scene will do what it's done over the last forty years and just kind of run itself by being a subculture. Realistically, the ball scene isn't really steered by any particular person. There's no written laws, there's no rules in place, it's just like a hurricane in the ocean....It's just spinning uncontrollably."

I planted myself directly in front of the scrutinizing judges, turning my head from side to side so they could see that my face had no flaws (if only due to the severe makeup application). The judges casually gave me my tens, nodding their heads as the emcee declared, "Tens! Tens! Tens! Tens across the board!" I breathed and stood to the side, waiting for more competition.

There were ten others who competed for New Face of the Year. I walked again with three other boys and won. I was surprised I'd made it that far, thinking I wouldn't get past the first set of beautiful boys. Finally it was down to three, including me and two others who were strikingly gorgeous. "The final three to the back of the runway," the emcee instructed. "Deejay, start the beat!" "Love Hangover" roared again as the three of us "sold our faces" down the runway. I placed my hands on the sides of my face, moving them up and down as if I were tracing a picture frame to emphasize my undeniable "carta." Once all three of us reached the panel, we were ordered to stand directly in front of the judges so they could see who was the "ovah-est of them all."

"Get up into it!" the emcee demanded. "Get into the skin, the teeth, the nose, the structure!" All three of us faced the judges, with me in the middle. The judges stood from their chairs, examining every detail of our faces. I heard one of the judges point out to the young man next to me, "Honey, that child has a chipped front tooth. That's not face, darling!" I gave a beaming smile and traced my index finger over my straight teeth.

The frenzied crowd surrounded us, hollering out who they thought the winner should be. I soaked in the attention, throwing my head back with a cocky grin. "Who do you see?" the emcee asked, pointing to the judges as they announced their choice. I wanted to win, not only to be a "ballroom diva," but to feel and believe that I was good at something. I needed to be adored by someone. As I stared into the eyes of the judges, every insecurity and negative thought flooded into the most delicate part of my soul.

I lost New Face of the Year, and that was the last time I participated in the ballroom scene. I admired it from afar and respected it; as a black gay man, the ballroom is my history. The ballroom scene dates back as far as the 1920s, in the days of the Harlem Renaissance. White drag queens excluded black drag queens from pageants; therefore, black drag queens started their own pageants. Over the years, the balls would evolve, and the early drag queen competitions came to include categories for every part of the black and Latin LGBT community. In this ball-shaped world, we manically strive to be iconic; everyone wants to be famous. To be a celebrity. To be a legend.

We owe thanks to pioneers like Paris Dupree, Crystal LaBeija, Pepper LaBeija, Dorian Corey, Avis Pendavis, Kevin Ultra-Omni, Willi Ninja, and countless nameless, faceless others who debuted dance moves appropriated by pop stars, slang stolen by campy reality television personalities, and style branded by fashion designers. More than anything, I value the lessons the ballroom scene taught me: to show confidence even at my most insecure, create something out of nothing, and *always* make it happen.

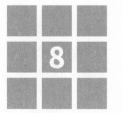

THE HIP-HOP
CLOSET

AS A BLACK MAN, HIP-HOP SAVED ME. HIP-HOP WAS MY
Black Twitter. Hip-hop was my Black Lives Matter. As I was growing up
in the 1990s, songs like 2Pac's "Holler If Ya Hear Me," Nas's "The World
Is Yours," and The Notorious B.I.G.'s "Juicy" tapped into my angst. Trying to survive West Philadelphia and rarely seeing representations of my
community in media, hearing my story chronicled in music was crucial to
survival. Undoubtedly, hip-hop is one of the most precious, creative, and
iconic forms of art black Americans created. As someone from the hip-hop
generation, I am grateful for artists like Ice Cube, Q-Tip, KRS-One, Brand
Nubian, and Common—all artists who proudly spat hateful, anti-LGBT
lyrics.

As a gay man, hip-hop hurt me. I remember when I first heard Ice
Cube's homophobic anthem "No Vaseline," which was Cube claiming his
former group members of N.W.A., who were now his enemies, were all
getting fucked by men. The track was and still is considered a classic diss
record, but when I listened to the 1991 song, and countless others, I knew
there was no place for my identities in hip-hop. Dr. Dre's *The Chronic*
is on my list of top five hip-hop albums, but nearly the entire record is
Dre and Snoop telling all their enemies to suck their dicks—an attack on
their manhood. Much like women who grapple with sexism in hip-hop,
I was taught to deal with the blows; this was the artists' "reality," and I
had to separate the music from the madness. However, LGBT identity and
hip-hop are not mutually exclusive. I am still a black man grappling with

police brutality, a crumbling education system, lack of jobs, and the struggle of day-to-day survival. The music of the streets simultaneously loved and shamed me.

A classic example of hip-hop's love and shame is Hot 97's Mister Cee, a legendary deejay in New York City, accused of allegedly (and repeatedly) soliciting male and transgender female sex workers. Cee, forty-six at the time, was a native New Yorker with roots in the West Indies. He worked with giants in hip-hop like Big Daddy Kane and The Notorious B.I.G. Cee is a stereotypically masculine man in hip-hop. Therefore, an allegation of same-sex or transgender relations dropped some jaws, because—bizarrely— people still believe sexual orientation is equivalent to gender expression. In reality, mannerisms do not dictate sexuality. There are plenty of masculine men who identify as gay, and there are masculine women who are heterosexual.

In May of 2013, the rumors became impossible to ignore; he was caught on tape soliciting sex from a self-proclaimed drag queen, which was reported by several major news outlets. Cee went on Hot 97 to discuss the controversy. For over forty minutes, Cee endured a verbal witch-hunt from his radio colleagues. He was interviewed by Ebro Darden, who was seemingly less concerned with the illegal activity of prostitution and dramatically and repeatedly demanded to know if Cee was gay—as if he were accusing the deejay of murder. Supposedly to soften the blow, Darden added, "We're going to crack some jokes because you're our brother."

To mock Cee further, another deejay, Cipha Sounds, played the house anthem "Follow Me," a song known for its popularity in gay clubs. Listening to the program, I thought to myself: If Cee is gay, embarrassing him and demanding the truth are not helpful. Who would shout they were "here and queer" during an interview like the one on Hot 97?

Clearly mocking their "brother" in crisis, the hosts sprinkled a little "We don't care if you're gay" babble—but they did care, and seemed to be enjoying interrogating Mister Cee, soaking up the glow of their "exclusive interview." Cee sounded desperate, confused, and he weakly attempted to explain himself personally and legally. It was sad to hear, but this was the culture of hip-hop I knew, constantly prepared to shatter the fragility of masculinity.

Sure, anti-gay sentiments aren't what they used to be in hip-hop. Eminem, 50 Cent, Common, and others no longer spit hateful lyrics. The rhymes may have changed, but the mindset has not. Yes, there is Frank Ocean, but he never used the word "gay" to describe his sexual orientation, and he gets a pass for his alternative quirkiness. Hot 97's tabloid interview with Cee proved there wasn't a safe space to come out in mainstream hip-hop.

In a candid moment of the interview, Cee calmly explained, "For argument's sake, let's say...if I'm lying. If I'm lying and I choose not to come out—that's my choice." Unhappy with the hypothetical, Ebro tried to shame Cee into confessing by claiming, "It's disrespectful to other gay and lesbian people because they see it as you're hiding something!" He added Cee not coming out "angers" people. When did Ebro become an expert on queer theory? Obviously Ebro isn't familiar with Keith Boykin's *One More River to Cross* or Alan Downs's *Velvet Rage*.

The LGBT community believes in freedom. "Coming out" is an individual journey, and contrary to what radio jocks on Hot 97 believe, unless you are outwardly homophobic, the LGBT community is not angry with anyone for not being out and proud. There might be folks who question why so-and-so isn't public, but it's a decision everyone must make in their own time. Dragging someone out of the closet can cause a lifetime of damage. Furthermore, many people have same-sex relations, but do not identify as gay, lesbian or as part of the LGBT community. Identities are fluid, complex, and not easily explained on radio airwaves. The toxic atmosphere of Hot 97's radio show was regressive and crude, and—if Mister Cee is not heterosexual—he was pushed deeper into the so-called closet.

Whether Cee is gay, bisexual, or doesn't believe in labels, I know many like him: A forty-six-year-old black man who grew up without today's affirmations and with the restraints of hip-hop. Twenty years older than Frank Ocean, over a decade older than Jason Collins, Cee and many in his generation are not inclined to identify under the LGBT umbrella. Mister Cee is compelled to be closeted through society's pressure to perform masculinity.

Thankfully, Mister Cee never spat homophobia; he repeatedly said he embraced the LGBT community. Living an authentic life delivers incredible blessings—on your terms. Cee is allowed to identify however he desires without justification. What if he is straight? Then the hot-button word "gay" is once again being used to criminalize black male sexuality.

Ironically, Cee's Hot 97 radio cohorts claimed to support the LGBT community, but with their catty jokes and "tranny" one-liners, they were ignorantly manifesting homophobia, a concept clearly lost in their insular bubble.

Wading the muddy waters of sexuality is overwhelming, especially if you're in the fairy-tale land of "manly" hip-hop, which worships flashy cars, barely legal "beauties," and imaginary big dicks.

Being gay is still the greatest insult you can hurl at someone in hip-hop. In November 2015, Vivica A. Fox said her ex, 50 Cent, was a "booty snatcher" because of the way he posed on a magazine cover with Soulja Boy. Social media went wild: Viv, who is allegedly an ally of the LGBT community, was using sexual orientation to insult her ex from more than a decade ago—and it worked. 50 defended himself by calling the *Independence Day* actress every variation of *bitch* and *hoe*. When Drake and Meek Mill feuded in July of 2015, Drake's major insult was claiming that Meek was the "wife" of Nicki Minaj, a takedown of Meek's manhood. Masculinity is the ultimate goal in hip-hop.

As a child and teenager, I worshipped the hypermasculine men of hip-hop. If I only possessed the grimy swagger of Ol' Dirty Bastard, the rugged masculinity of Treach from Naughty by Nature, or the intimidation skills of anyone in N.W.A., I believed I could survive West Philadelphia or any other city. As I walked the streets, I listened to songs like Method Man's "Bring the Pain," hoping the track would inject me with the niggahood I could never achieve. I studied the drug dealers on corners, wondering what magic tricks I needed to become one of them. The pressure of black masculinity overwhelmed every aspect of my pre-adult life, with hip-hop as one of the main ingredients. I longed to be wholly included in the narrative of hip-hop.

Hip-hop embraced materialism, violence, and capitalism, but rejected me. Thankfully, I found freedom in the sounds of the black LGBT community, and unless it was a Queen Latifah or Lauryn Hill, I abandoned the music of my streets. No one in hip-hop was rapping about being black and LGBT. However, house music, in its unique way, tackled identities in songs like "10,000 Screaming Faggots" by the Moonwalkers featuring Ultra Naté, "You Don't Even Know Me" by Armand Van Helden, and "How You Wanna Carry It" by Baltimore's Miss Tony. The LGBT clubs were an escape from hip-hop, with gender nonconforming, proudly femme, overtly masculine, and transgender people mingling under the big tent of house music—zero judgment, just freedom dancing.

One of the most famous black LGBT clubs in New York City during the late 1990s and early 2000s was the Warehouse in the Bronx. The space was an actual warehouse, with hip-hop music on a small first floor that was usually empty, and nonstop house music on the spacious second floor, consistently packed with people dancing their soul away. Patrons traveled from all over to the Warehouse, deep in the Bronx, on a Friday or Saturday night for soulful house music. However, I gradually noticed a shift: The house floor began to play thirty or so minutes of hip-hop each night. The energy and look of the club transitioned; people who I had once seen in semi-drag were now rocking a hat cocked to the side, heavy jewelry, cornrows, and baggy clothes. Masculinity was worshipped in a way I usually saw from heterosexual men. Dancing in the club to house music was no longer cool; it was effeminate. If you wanted to be considered attractive or desirable, anything slightly femme was a turnoff. The roles reversed: One night I walked into the Warehouse with a group of friends and the hip-hop was upstairs on the huge floor with the house music regulated to the tiny first floor. One of my friends, who was what we called a "house head," who loved his deep rhythms and tribal beats, prophesized, "This is the beginning of the end for our clubs. Hip-hop has taken over the gays." Everyone sashayed in homo-thug drag, performing masculinity, no matter how inauthentic.

The black LGBT clubs that once embraced drag queens and trans people now shunned anyone who didn't match a pseudo-thug environment. I heard comments like, "Why are all these trannies in here? This isn't a tranny club" from black gay men. I saw promoters refusing trans women at the door with excuses: "There are too many of you in here. Come back next week, boo." Black gay clubs were no longer a safe space for transgender women. Ironically, if it weren't for trans women of color specifically fighting for equality decades ago, LGBT clubs would still be illegal in many cities across the country.

Legendary house deejays complained no one booked them for clubs if they didn't spin hip-hop. A piece of our culture was dying: house music specifically for the black LGBT community. By the early 2000s, house was considered effeminate and old. Hip-hop was masculine and young. Both statements were lies. Within a few years, nearly every house club from New York to Washington, D.C., closed their doors, including the Warehouse. Hip-hop bulldozed over house music.

I am grateful to have had the experiences of house music in the LGBT community before hip-hop took over. In many ways, hip-hop has no place for me or people like me, but I can never fully abandon the music of my youth. I appreciate artists and still hold them accountable for their sexism or homophobia. I fought against the hypermasculine trappings of hip-hop.

Today, homophobia in hip-hop is no longer profitable. Rappers say they support the LGBT community, but who knows if they really support us or if they are afraid of the wrath that can demolish careers. The mindset doesn't appear to have shifted. Many LGBT hip-hop artists are shut out of record labels, radio airplay, and profit. Until I see a black LGBT person fully exist in hip-hop, the way an Elton John, Wanda Sykes, or Ellen DeGeneres can in their fields, then I will stop giving alleged progression in hip-hop the side-eye.

INSECURE

IN MY TWENTIES, I WAS NEVER COMFORTABLE OWNING MY sexual orientation. I wasn't "closeted" or lying, but as a matter of safety, I was quiet. In college, in my neighborhood, and at work, I maintained my silence. In the deepest of my insecurities—and I'm not proud to admit this—it was an ego boost when a straight woman believed I was hetero. Many gay men will proudly brag, "Women still hit on me," as if it's a badge of pseudo-hetero honor. In reality, it's an internal sigh of relief, which says, "I can still pass for straight." The feeling connects back to standards of manhood, haunting many men, regardless of their sexual orientation. It takes years of work to remember, believe, and own that your sexuality does not make you less or more of a man. Existing as who you truly are makes you the greatest man you can be, regardless of sexual orientation. If only men were taught this as little boys.

I've been rejected by the best of them, so I admire anyone who boldly walks up to a stranger and makes their interest clear. When I am approached by straight women, I am careful to be respectful, kind, and gentlemanly. However, I am clueless when anyone finds me attractive. I quickly assume, "I'm not their type." Coy flirting, playing games, and throwing subliminal messages never translate to me. I need clarity, a clear "Do you want to go out on a date?" Tina, a young woman I met in college, wasn't clear, and I was clueless.

Tina was regal with her sharp features, tall and thin stature, and shapely body. She was fascinating to watch in class, answering questions or in a heated debate with another student. She was a goddess; a mix of Iman and Anita Hill. She aspired to go into politics, which was easy to envision. Conversations with her consistently made me challenge my thinking on race, gender, and politics. Tina was "woke." Plenty of men had crushes on her, and she could clearly land any man on campus, but, strangely, she developed a connection to me.

Tina suggested we study together for an intense literature class. I immediately agreed; I learned better with a partner, and with Tina's help, I might earn an A, I thought. We began studying and bonding, I assumed as friends. We soon exchanged numbers, but after three study sessions, I noticed Tina was flirting, wearing skintight shirts, falling into my lap, and finding any opportunity to touch me. You might wonder why I didn't simply tell her I was gay. I detested the insinuation that LGBT people are required to explain their identity to heterosexuals, especially in the early 2000s, when LGBT issues were still taboo. I enrolled in college to learn, not to teach beginning courses on sexual orientation. In addition, like most people in their early twenties, I didn't possess the language to explain my evolving identity. But I never flirted back, never engaged, and, eventually, canceled further study sessions to avoid mixed messages.

After I canceled our third study session, Tina started calling me incessantly on my landline. My best friend Nikki and I were living together. I begged her, "Answer the phone for me! Say I'm not home."

"Why? Just tell her you aren't interested."

"I don't feel like explaining. Put the phone on speaker, but hold the phone up close so she doesn't know. Please!"

Nikki rolled her eyes and answered in her sex-kitten voice, "Hello?"

"Don't talk like that!" I hissed in her ear.

She covered the speaker. "Hush! She might be part lesbian!"

"Is Clay there?" Tina asked.

"No, he's not here. May I ask who's calling?"

"This is Tina. Who is this?" she snapped with an attitude.

"This is his roommate," Nikki quietly answered.

"Roommate? Why would you be his roommate?"

I mouthed, "Oh, Lord!" to Nikki.

"We live together, Tina."

"Why are you getting an attitude with me?" Tina spat.

"I'm not getting an attitude with you," Nikki calmly replied, balling a fist at me.

"Yes, you are! I don't appreciate it!"

"Girl!" Nikki said. I put my face in my hands. "You need to calm down."

"I'm not trying to get with your boyfriend!" Tina now yelled.

"He's not my boyfriend!" Nikki shot back. I waved my hands, begging Nikki to stay calm.

"Really? Are you his maid?"

Nikki got her neck roll on, losing her cool. "Honey! He's fucking gay!"

I threw my hands in the air, mouthing, "Just hang up!"

"What?"

"Yes, gay! Fucking gay! Like, sucks dick gay!"

Tina hung up.

"Nikki!" I screamed. "What the fuck? Now she's going to tell everyone in class. Damn!"

"Child, you're a grown-ass man. I'm not gonna argue with some crazy straight girl over you. Why do you even care?"

"Because! It's not your call to tell her what I am," I insisted. "You basically outed me!"

"Boy, please. Don't pull that on me. It's not your call to put me on the phone with Miss *Fatal Attraction* and expect me to not react." The phone rang again. "Answer it!" Nikki demanded, shoving the phone at me.

"Fuck!" I said, taking the phone. "Hello?"

"Clay? It's Tina," said a calm voice. "Are you gay?"

I sighed. Honestly, this scenario wasn't Nikki's fault. There's no winning, even in the smallest of circumstances, when you're striving to be inauthentic. Tina was smart, logical, and conscious, and we spent a chunk of the semester together, working hard to ace the class. I needed to give her more credit. *I can't presume everyone will shut me down because of who I sleep with*, I thought. She knew me beyond my sexuality, which was the key to combating stereotypes. She saw me before my sexuality.

"Yes, I am gay, Tina. I didn't say anything because—"

"Fag!" she quickly snapped, then gave me the dial tone.

"What happened?" Nikki asked as I stared at the phone in my hand.

"She called me a fag and hung up," I answered, a little stunned.

"That bitch!" Nikki exclaimed.

Tina never spoke to me again.

These days, I obviously wouldn't hesitate to tell someone that I'm gay, but everyone deserves their process—which reminds me of the last time I attended CBGB in New York City's pre-gentrification East Village in 2005.

Punk-rock goddess Tamar-kali was performing. None of my R&B friends wanted to sit through a rock show, so I trekked there by myself. Arriving a little early, not recognizing a soul in the room, I casually walked around CBGB, admiring the grit of the soon-to-be-closed venue. A young woman locked eyes with me. With a slightly terrifying presence, like the opening of a *Dateline ID* episode, her stare was intense, lips parted and eyes wide. A little unnerved by her glare, I nodded back with a smile.

She motioned for me to come closer. I reluctantly walked over as she put her hand out for me to shake. "You're cute!" she complimented me in a husky voice. I laughed nervously and thanked her for the kind words, getting a better visual. She was a thick, tall girl with so much makeup I envisioned her dipping her face in a bowl of light-brown chocolate frosting. Her lips were decorated with blood-red lipstick and she tossed around a head of lovely locs down to her shoulders, an odd contrast to the pounds of makeup.

"Who are you here with?" she quizzed.

"By myself."

"Really? Do you have a girlfriend?" Her eyes spread over her face like two tablespoons of butter on pancakes.

I answered honestly, "No, I don't have a girlfriend." Her eyeballs melted as she asked my name.

"Well, I'm single and my name is Mandy," she responded, softly batting her eyelashes. I didn't know her story, but I could imagine she had been hurt before, like all of us. She craved love, and each person she met could be a potential husband. I understood her emotional hunger, even as she grilled me in an intense interview session.

"Where are you from? Where do you live? Zodiac? College?" After the interrogation, she confirmed again that I didn't have a girlfriend. I told her no, laughing as I answered.

Mandy snapped back with, "Yeah, you look like you need some pussy." I thought, *You don't know the half of it, love juice!*

"Really? Why do you say that?" I asked, knowing I was getting into dangerous territory.

"I can just tell. My coochie is really good." This made my jaw drop—a reaction that's nearly impossible to get out of me. I am usually unshockable.

"Really?"

She stared me down like I was challenging her worth. "Yes. It smells like mangoes!"

"Mangoes?"

"Yes, and I make the best mango pancakes. I'd like to make them for you!" I was struggling to contain myself, wondering if I should tell her I wasn't hetero. Her powerful energy intimidated me. I chuckled uncomfortably as she took my laugh as a signal to fall all over me and mash her bosom in my face. Her bosom did, I tell no lies, smell like fresh mangoes on a tree in the islands. She continued poking her breasts at me and throwing her head back with wild laughs. I was waiting for her to tear off her denim skirt, wrap her legs around my neck, and slam her mango coochie in my face. I attempted to reclaim my personal space and asked, "So, why don't you have a boyfriend?"

She quickly replied, like she had been waiting for the question since the moment we met, "Because I'm the best girlfriend in the world!"

"How so?"

"I don't mind if my boyfriend fucks around—as long as he tells me."

"Really?" I was thinking, *That isn't being the best girlfriend in the world; that's just low self-esteem.* "Does that mean you can fuck around, too?" I asked.

"No!" she corrected me, as if she might have ruined her chances to cook me mango pancakes. "I'm a serial monogamist and women just can't do that." I almost wanted to explore that comment, but I knew that would get me into overly revealing ground with Mandy.

Tamar-kali was about to perform and I wanted to absorb the rock goddess without talk of mangoes. Mandy gave me her number and questioned, "Are you gonna call me? I really want to make you those pancakes!"

That was my opportunity to say I was not one of the straights, but why should I? Why should I explain myself to the mango goddess? I lied and said I would call. She was satisfied with my answer and stared at me throughout the night. As I enjoyed Tamar-kali's godlike performing, Mandy strutted over to me and whispered in my ear, "I can't wait to lick your yellow goodness." If I wore pearls, I would've clutched them.

The last time I saw Mandy, she was dancing to the hardcore soul-punk music, swinging her head back and forth, popping her body to the rhythms. I remember saying to myself, "She dances just like Molly Ringwald in *The Breakfast Club* on the staircase in the library!" I never called Mandy. However, I was impressed by her fearless attitude, although I couldn't decipher whether the root of it was liberation or desperation. I could imagine Mandy waiting for my call with the pancakes on the griddle and her "coochie" freshly marinated with mangoes.

I don't have the freedom of approaching anyone I find attractive and feeling entitled to have them. I only approach men in safe spaces. I've locked eyes with straight men and quickly got a "What the fuck are you looking at?" Tina, who called me a fag when I revealed I was gay, and Mandy, who approached me vagina first, weren't concerned with explanations about their sexual orientation. Perceived access to anyone you think is cute or attractive is a privilege. However, now I realize that saying I am not heterosexual isn't a simple explanation; it's claiming my rightful space, which is liberating. This experience is true for any of us who are forced to reconcile the social realities surrounding our identities.

I am rarely hit on by straight women today, which I know doesn't indicate anything about my manhood. When you step into your true self, you dodge the trappings of inauthenticity. All these years later, though, I wonder if I missed an opportunity to indulge in Mandy's specialty pancakes and a coochie that smelled like mangoes. A few mimosas and my "yellow goodness" could've obliged.

LOVE

I WILL
REMEMBER YOU

MY EYES WERE FIXED ON A LONG, NEON GREEN LIZARD planted on the wall outside of First Caribbean National Bank in Montego Bay, Jamaica. The reptile blended into the shrubbery, but it caught my attention as I was waiting for Carson. With one quick movement, the lizard could easily vanish, as chameleons do. I was afraid the lizard might spring from the wall and attack me, but I couldn't resist being mesmerized by a species you would never see in New York City. The more I stared, the more beautiful the lizard became. Its eyes were a bright turquoise, the skin glowed, and its shape was sleek, animated like something from a Pixar film. I slowly put my fingers out, hoping to touch the lizard, but the doors of the bank swung open and I heard "Clay!" in a thick Jamaican accent. The lizard dashed away.

After months of chatting online, I was finally seeing Carson in person. His wide smile, deep-set eyes, clean-shaven face, and strong jawline shook my soul. He was even more attractive in the flesh. Carson put his hand out for me to shake. I wondered why I didn't get a hug, or at least the standard "dude" hug—shake of the hand, then dive in for a quick pat on the back. Then I remembered I was in Jamaica. It was July of 2005; the island hadn't been named the most homophobic place on the planet by *TIME* magazine just yet—that would happen in 2006—but Jamaica's reputation for anti-gay sentiment was legendary.

In 1992, Buju Banton documented Jamaica's violent homophobia with the crowd pleaser "Boom Bye Bye," a dancehall track that advocated for the burning, shooting, and killing of anyone who did not fit into the rigid constructs of male-female gender roles. Who can forget Beenie Man's hateful signature song from 2002, "Bad Man Chi Chi Man," meaning "bad queer man"? Beenie enthusiastically encouraged his audience to kill gays, but Jamaica's homophobia wasn't limited to pop culture rants: A year before I arrived, in 2004, a father encouraged a schoolyard mob to attack his son, whom he believed was gay. The teen's fellow students tore boards from benches and beat him until he was unconscious. He was in the eleventh grade. Supposedly, his father watched with a smile.

When I arrived in Montego Bay, Jamaica, in July of 2005, it was the most beautiful place I had ever seen. Living as I did in the concrete savagery of New York City, the green and blue of the island mesmerized me. The air was clear, the people were strikingly beautiful, and in some strange way, which could've been my own American privilege, I felt a sense of home in Jamaica.

I had been video chatting for months with Carson, who I met in an LGBT Jamaican chat room. I told him I was traveling to Montego Bay and promised we would meet. I was hesitant because it was Jamaica. *Was this a possible set up to trap a gay tourist?* I thought. However, when he invited me to meet at his job at the First Caribbean National Bank, and we locked eyes, I knew I was safe. We ate at Island Grill during his lunch break with a thick intensity between us. His eyes felt like heat on my face. "Don't stare too hard. I don't want to get us killed," I half-joked.

"Don't worry. I'm smart. I won't get you in no trouble," he flirted with a wink. We talked for the full hour about Jamaica, America, music, movies, and all things pop culture. As I walked him back to his job, he said, "Wow. That was a good conversation. I never get to talk to someone like this. I'm always pretending." Carson's story might sound like the cliché of a pitiful closeted man, but his journey was complicated with the nuances of family, his island, and, like the lizard, the requirement to be a chameleon: If you are found out, you must run.

Why is Jamaica so deeply and proudly homophobic? The obvious answer would be religion. Regardless of the stereotypes of marijuana use, steamy dance halls, and island rendezvous, Jamaica is heavily Christian with a legacy of colonization. Examining Jamaica historically, however, oppressive legislation, like "buggery laws"—also known as sodomy laws—applied to heterosexuals as well. These oppressive rules were colonial laws passed down from the British, not rooted in the culture from the people. The Brits eventually abolished these statutes, but the Jamaican government selectively embraced the colonizer's rules. Artists like Beenie Man, and even Jamaica's former Prime Minister, Orette Bruce Golding, argue that homophobia is synonymous with Jamaica. On the contrary: Jamaicans are not adhering to Jamaican culture; the country is adhering to colonized culture—oppressive and dated rules that did not originate in Africa.

A sixty-minute lunch with Carson wasn't enough. I needed to see more of him. He agreed to come to my hotel after work. A few hours later I was face-to-face with him again in the lobby of the hotel. "Have you been in the ocean yet?" was the first thing he asked with a wide smile.

"No, I just got here yesterday."

"You gotta extra pair of shorts?"

Carson and I splashed in the clear, warm, blue water, keeping our safe distance. You never knew who was watching. He swam like a fish, laughing that I couldn't go underwater without holding my nose. The sounds we made as our bodies treaded through the ocean echoed like a melody. His head shined as he laughed with Jamaica's red-and-orange sun setting behind him, framing his face. The extreme heat, the epic ocean, the sizzling sun, and the lush colors that were nonexistent in grim New York almost made me ignore something on Carson's finger that flashed in the sun, winking at me, insisting that it be seen.

"Is that a wedding ring?" I questioned as he dipped his hand back in the clear water.

"Yeah, man, it is," he answered with his head bowed.

"You didn't tell me you were married," I said angrily.

"I know," he admitted, still not looking at me. "It's hard."

"Carson, you're a nice guy, but spare me the 'man on the down low' speech," I snapped, ready for him to leave.

"No, man, it's different than that. I just didn't have no choice."

"We all have choices."

"You ain't Jamaican. I didn't want to put my life on the line to be gay. You can't get a job. You're an embarrassment to your family. It might be hard in America, but I've seen friends stabbed, killed, set on fire and nobody cared. I promised myself, I wouldn't die like that. Every gay man in Jamaica is married. If you're not married, you're living on the streets."

He grabbed my hand under the water, slipped off his wedding ring, and placed the ring on my finger. He told a story that I heard many times before. He wanted to get to know me. He believed he could get to know me. He told me all those things you say when you are excited about a new face. I wondered how many men heard this monologue. I felt him, but I couldn't receive him, though his accent danced in my head. He was so beautiful.

Even if you believe the argument that homophobia is the fabric of Jamaica, that does not mean hate is acceptable. Not all things that are part of "culture" are positive. Black Americans protested against white Southern culture, which relished in dehumanizing them through music, literature, film, and policy. This hate was protected by the government in the name of culture. Yes, I know some will object to the insinuation that there is any link between homophobia and racism. The truth is, all forms of oppression—sexism, racism, homophobia, anti-Semitism—have a link. You cannot advocate for an end to racism but still be a proponent of homophobia.

Furthermore, why the outrage against lesbian, gay, bisexual, and transgender people in Jamaica? Gays in Jamaica are not the cause of mass corruption in the government. Lesbians in Jamaica cannot be blamed for the epic drug trade. Sexuality and gender should be a nonissue for the people of Jamaica. Even so, every government needs a scapegoat to make itself appear as if it is properly serving the people.

I was nervous to bring Carson back to my hotel room, but he needed to change into his dry clothes. I was seriously attracted to him and terrified of touching a married man. In America, if a man told me he was married, I instantly cut off communication, but my heart and mind weren't in sync on the beautiful island. At my core, I wanted to spend more time with him. I didn't want him to vanish and never see him again.

We walked into the hotel room and I quickly ran for his clothes. "You can change in the bathroom."

"Why are you rushing me out?" he asked.

"Because you are married, Carson. I hear what you're saying about your life and everything, but you're a married man. I just can't—"

"Is that a balcony?" he interrupted, walking past me, opening the balcony door. "Wow, this is nice, up here high. They don't let the locals in a place like this. Come out here."

"Carson, I think you should head home."

"Clay." He turned around, Jamaica's night sky outlining his frame as he stood shirtless in damp shorts. "Just sit out here for a minute and I'll leave. You'll never see me again. Give me a moment."

I hesitantly walked to the balcony. The sky was beautiful; all I could see were palm trees, stars, and the ocean. We sat in plastic chairs as he wrapped his callused fingers over mine. I laughed, putting my head in my other hand.

"What's wrong?"

"You're married."

"Entrapment. Not married. If I had a choice, I would be with someone like you."

Carson wasn't an evil character from a Tyler Perry film. He was a man who knew his life was at risk if he ever attempted to be his authentic self. I asked, "Why not move to Europe or the States? You shouldn't have to live like this, especially if you feel so trapped."

He calmly answered, "This is *my* island. This is where my family is. I love my island. I deserve to be here like anyone else. I don't want to run somewhere else to be gay." I couldn't argue with that.

We sat on the balcony, holding hands, our conversation shifting back to pop culture and music. He showed me his iPod and I scrolled through his music; the majority of the songs were Madonna, Celine Dion, and Barbra Streisand. "Your wife doesn't know you're gay with all this butch queen music?" I teased.

"Celine's 'The Power of Love' was our wedding song!" he laughed.

"Oh, Lord! Did you lip-synch the song in drag, too?" I laughed.

"I have a request!" he said with excitement.

"I'm not slow dancing with you to Celine Dion!" I snapped.

"Stand up!" He jumped to his feet, his hand still wrapped in mine.

"What are you doing?" I complained, standing up, matching his height. Carson released my hand, wrapped his hand around the back of my neck, pulled me into him, and kissed me. He put every bit of his soul into that kiss as our bare chests touched. He pulled his entire body into mine; his heart pounded through his chest, and the kiss vibrated through me. I began spinning down a dangerous rabbit hole. My insides sizzled, but I felt the wedding ring as his fingers caressed the small of my back. I pulled away. We stared. His eyes were red, lips parted, and body sweaty.

"I never kissed a man outside." Tears welled up in his eyes. He squeezed my biceps. "You'll be gone in a few days. You'll forget about me. Don't think I don't have morals. Don't think I don't know I'm wrong. I know, I know." I hugged him. He rested his head on my shoulder and sobbed from his gut.

His tears fell down my back. "This is how it should feel. It should feel real. I don't feel real."

Carson was like the lizard, undoubtedly beautiful, but never having lived in the freedom of his true colors. If he couldn't blend in, his life was in danger. There was no sanctuary.

"I will remember you," I whispered in his ear.

I never saw Carson again.

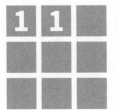

AVERY

5/27 2:00 p.m.

Avery. I met him a week ago today. He is an actor on Broadway. We had an amazing date on Sunday. He stayed the night on Wednesday. He sent me a text when he got to work and I wasn't expecting that. He said he would call me last night, but he never did. I'm waiting for his call today. Waiting on another person to call. I hate that I still do this—I just met the man but I'm looking for validation already. I need a certain amount of attention to feel secure. People are so fleeting; you think they like you but they do vanishing acts. Now I am analyzing everything. He wasn't very affectionate in the morning. Maybe I'm just looking for something wrong. I treat people well and I expect to be treated the same. A simple phone call can give you reassurance. I keep looking at the clock.

On Monday he didn't call either. The next day we talked and he explained his phone died. I overreacted. Could be overreacting now. Any hint of anything less than perfect scares me. As I told Avery, I just want a fair chance to get to know him. He said I remind him of a guy he fell in love with who died in a car crash when he was a teenager. Someone I knew of recently passed away. I hope he was able to find love. I hope he felt security in love for a long period of time at one point in his thirty years. I hope Avery doesn't dislocate my heart.

5/30 12:15 a.m.

Wow. Just see what I have put myself through with relationships. All the self-doubt, the rejection that isn't even real, conjuring up scenarios and overanalyzing every moment. I need to stay in the fucking moment. Avery is proof. Things have been good with Avery. On Saturday afternoon, at about five-thirty, we had an incredible lunch date. We talked about Broadway, dating, how his best friend said "the writer," meaning me, was rubbing off on him, making him speak better on stage. We laughed so much as I walked him back to the theater. He stressed that he liked me, that he could be in a relationship with me. He offered to give me a tour of the show. I was hoping he would offer. We entered through a brown stage door, and to the left were building staffers who greeted Avery with a head nod. A dancer walked in and Avery immediately introduced me. I felt like he was making an effort to incorporate me into his life. We took the elevator up and I just couldn't believe that he was taking me to this space. This was his world.

We got off the elevator and we were backstage. Everything was black and brown. He walked me onto the stage and I stood in the middle. It took my breath away to see all of the red seats, knowing in less than an hour they would be filled. I saw the crevasses in the floor, indicating what would move. He explained how the stage is thirty feet deep. It was inspiring. It looked so small but I knew dreams were made on that stage. He took me to his dressing room. It was a dark room with a red and orange tint. He showed me his wardrobe. The soft lights on the mirror of his dresser made my eyes hurt if I stared too long. On our way out, he took me to the basement where he warms up and sometimes calls me before going on stage. This was my dream, to kiss him at his Broadway show. He leaned me up against the aged, pale peach wall and gave me soft kisses with smiles in between. We were both nervous about someone coming by. I could hear the echo of our kisses in the stairwell.

We returned to the stage door, making small talk as more cast members walked by. He said one of these days I could meet him after the show, which I've already imagined. He said that his cast members would look at me, giving me the eye, asking about me, and he would say, "That's my man." When I walked away he was still looking in my direction. I waved back. I was so elated that I walked from Forty-Eighth and Broadway to Fifteenth and Eighth Avenue. I played Katy Perry's "Teenage Dream" on repeat. I got a text from a friend saying, "Hey, just saw you smiling down Eighth Avenue." I laughed because I hadn't realized I was beaming while walking down the street. I was high on my time with him. Like something out of a movie. It was only one hour and forty-five minutes.

6/2 12:00 a.m.

Avery stayed the night. We had one of those New York City summer dates that filled the whole day. I loved walking next to him. I cherished turning a corner and finding him there. He said that I "stop a room." He came back to my house and commented on how attentive I was and how he has never been with someone so attentive. I believe he's sincerely interested in me. I try to stay in the moment, but there are so many moments. They say, "Be present!" He's so beautiful that it's hard not to see beyond one moment. His smile, slightly crooked teeth, and muscular frame with a healthy amount of fat. He lights me up by how he laughs with his whole face. Everything is so perfect now. Will he be able to ride when it's not pretty?

6/7 12:30 a.m.

Last night, the teenage dream got a little real. He got some alcohol in his system and got a little ignorant—confessional but ignorant. Had me waiting for fifteen minutes outside of Madison Square Garden for a concert. He told me he was purposely late because he wanted to avoid seeing people he thought would be there—exes. That didn't sit well, but I didn't want to ruin the night. After the concert, we went to a party with his friends and he put me on display. Asking people what they thought my racial background was. I felt like a monkey in a cage. We eventually left the party and, again, I didn't bring up how uncomfortable I felt because I didn't want to damage the night. But Avery took a turn I didn't see coming. He babbled about not being "ready," meaning us, but he wanted "it," which scared me. I was confused. We talked about his fear again today and I got no answers. He apologized for being so confusing. I saw an obtrusive, intense side of Avery that I've never seen before. I guess the "not ready" rants were living in his head and I didn't even know. I just like him. I want to work at it. I'm tired of it not working out. He just called.

6/14 11:50 p.m.

Avery and I had sex last night, like, full-blown sex. It was beautiful. Now he wants to do me. Ugh. I'm not ready for that. Today he was a little cranky or just "off." He apologized. I went to three of his performances this week. Just supporting. I like him so much. It'll be four weeks soon. We made it almost thirty days and hopefully can make it more. On Saturday, he told me his gut instinct is telling him that we were meant to be together. I agreed and told him I don't believe in love at first sight and I'm not in love, but this is the closest I've been to it. I want him. I want him to fall in love with me.

6/23 1 p.m.

On Sunday, Avery and I had a moment over music—or maybe I should say he had one all by himself. My God! He got so upset because I am not a fan of the same music. He apologized for his attitude but good God, it was annoying. Avery can be very dramatic. He is a good guy though. I am just getting tired of the judgments on me—him saying I am not as free as him or how proper I am. In some ways it's a compliment but in other ways it's a sweeping character assessment.

6/27 8:30 p.m.

Yesterday with Avery was horrible. I saw a terrible person. As he described himself: a bitch and selfish. I would add *evil* and *illogical*. We were having dinner and I could tell he was irritable. He was rude to the server, complained about the heat, and couldn't find anything he liked on the menu. An attractive guy walked by and nodded at me. I nodded back, not sure if I knew him. For some bipolar reason, Avery snapped, "Hmph! I don't even know if you're seeing anyone else."

"Huh?" I was confused. "Are you mad because that guy nodded at me?"

"Everyone looks at you, you know that. You like it," he nearly growled. He appeared to be a different person. His facial muscles were tight, his posture was stiff, and his bright eyes were sharp, staring at me. I stressed how much I adored him and said I wasn't seeing anyone else. He continued, "I don't know that!" I asked where these accusations were coming from; he claimed he was being "realistic." As we were leaving the restaurant, I explained I felt like he was trying to start a fight.

He argued that I was judging him. "Why would you think I would pick a fight? What are you doing wrong?" I said he was insecure, and Avery lost his allegedly secure mind. He yelled, "Don't call me insecure again, my friend, or I'm going to get really upset. You're not perfect! You're not Jesus!" he said, pointing at me, his chest heaving. He appeared to be getting angrier because I was so calm; he stepped closer to me and, for a moment, I thought he might hit me.

"I'm leaving," I said, and he became a different person—he cracked; within seconds he was sobbing on the sidewalk. Shoulders shaking, tears pouring out of his eyes as passersby stared at me then shot eyes at him. I couldn't walk away. I held on to him. I tried to be understanding. He turned into Mr. Apology again. He was stressed over work and having a moment.

We were in New York's West Village. We found a quiet street and sat on a stoop; it looked like a movie set with a curved road, two-level houses, and dim streetlamps. Fireworks exploded above our heads, celebrating another year of LGBT Pride in the Big Apple. The fireworks were loud and bright, like bombs. But right now, Avery was the bomb.

It feels like he has a spell over me. I can't walk away just yet. Maybe he needs space to have his moment. I'm curious to see what the future will be. Will we get past this? Is this the real him? An insecure narcissist who will take out his rage on others who care for him? I want a healthy relationship, not craziness. All of our moments have been about his insecurities. He stomped on my heart and pleaded for forgiveness again. I hope he knows now how to do better.

6/30 11:40 p.m.

Avery was cruel but I'm choosing to move past it. I went to his house on Tuesday and he was the person I remembered. I helped him with two auditions. He might have landed both parts and he credited me for him doing so well. Thanked me a lot, which made me feel good. However, my insecurities popped up. All that ranting about if I'm seeing anyone else—I wonder if he is. I'm always afraid they will vanish on me. Tomorrow makes six weeks.

7/2 12:20 a.m.

He landed one of the roles! I knew it and felt he would get it. And he did. He deserves it. I'm happy for him as if I've been with him for years. I see big things for him and even bigger things for the both of us if we are together. I know that sounds intense, but as I told my BFF, I'm not in love but I can feel myself falling for him. I see him falling for me, too. Who knew when I looked at him that we could build something so strong. Wow….I am calling it strong. I'm in my head; accept the good, as I tell him.

7/5 11 p.m.

Avery and I are over. There was another blow-up last night, on the Fourth of July. He got ugly again. Up until that point, we had such a good time, despite some bickering—him being moody. There are so many details. His immaturity, cruelty; then he walked away from me on the street. Something I didn't do to him. Eventually, we got on the phone. After hours of yelling he finally calmed down. He said he "may not" be ready for a relationship but wanted to be in it.

We talked today. I asked if he still wanted to do this. He said he couldn't give me a clear answer. I was floored. I had been so supportive—going to shows, helping him rehearse, dealing with his mood swings, and accepting his apologies. But he can't tell me if he wants to work on it? He admitted to taking and not giving. He whined about me judging him even though a week ago he confessed, "You didn't judge me, I was the one judging myself and judging you." Forty minutes before he was to hit the stage—because that's when he called me—I made the decision, "Let's break up. I can't convince you that I'm not judging you. I've been treated better than this. You know you could've done better with how you treated me. If you think you can find someone who judges you less and is more supportive of you—then go on." All he said was, "Okay." About ten minutes later the phone rang again, but he hung up before I answered. I hoped he'd fight for it more. I don't think it will be the last time I'll hear from him. I really enjoyed my time. I thought it would work. He even said, "If you talked to me the way I talked to you, I wouldn't put up with that." I gave it my all, no matter what he put on me. Maybe that was my problem.

7/6 6:40 p.m.

He called and apologized for everything. He said that he tried, but he wasn't ready—even though he said he was ready on our first date. He said the demise of our relationship is his fault. He says he is in a selfish state; he needs to focus on his career or some BS. Maybe he doesn't have the tools to make a relationship or his career work. Here I am, hurt again, writing again. I thought I had it right this time.

7/11 11:30 p.m.

I haven't quite been able to let go. We talked yesterday and exchanged texts today. Don't ask me why I'm still entertaining him. He'll bring me nothing but down, but the heart wants what the heart wants.

7/14 10:00 p.m.

I tried so hard with Avery. I believed in him. I believed in us. I accepted the good. I thought we had a sane conversation. He brought up sex. I asked if we could both get tested for HIV. He got upset but didn't react until later, via text. He says he will never have sex with me again and that I don't respect or trust him. Huh? A new insult. I wrote him a text saying I couldn't believe he would say that to me. And if he cared anything about me he would not contact me again. I didn't mean to send it, but maybe it was divine intervention. I was praying to let go. The man twists things around like I've never seen. He said before that his mind "plays tricks" on him. I will sleep my love woes away tonight.

8/4 9 p.m.

Letting go of Avery has been hard. I believed it would work. But he went crazy on me. I felt so confident and happy with him. We had that unexplainable chemistry. It's awful to have chemistry with someone who isn't good for you, a cruel prank from the universe. I've met good, consistent, and kind people, but the chemistry wasn't there. Why do I have chemistry with this man? Out of all people.

8/7 11 p.m.

I wonder if he thinks of me more than I think of him. I wonder if he misses me. I just read through the past few months. I showed him the best part of myself, which is a disappointment. Avery has changed me. We weren't together for years, but this experience altered the way I view love. I'm not sure if this change is for the better. I learned that being beautiful isn't enough, chemistry isn't enough. These blues aren't worth it. I can't waste another millisecond on the Averys of the world. If someone of quality comes along and I'm with an Avery, I won't even know because I'll be focused on him, the wrong person. I need the road to be clear for the right person. I hope never to see Avery again. I'm sure I will. The universe is never that easy on me, but I'm going to be happy with someone. I have no doubts. I'm secure in the work I've done on myself. When it's my time, I'll be ready.

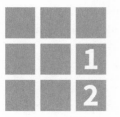

WARRIOR MARKS

I AM OFTEN ASKED, "WHAT WERE YOUR FAVORITE interviews?" The answer rarely involves a celebrity (unless we are talking about Patti LaBelle), but the stories that attach to my spirit, connect with my soul, and inspire me in my lowest moments, those interviews would be two unknowns: Simon and Donte. Their stories are vastly different, but exemplify the mighty struggle to exist through war, loss, sickness, and death.

In 1990, Simon was a senior in high school, seventeen years old, and living in an upper-middle-class area of Queensville, Liberia. His father and mother moved to America and were preparing all of their children to eventually move to the States. On Christmas Eve, 1989, an ominous sign of change hit Liberia. There was an uprising in the northernmost part of the country led by Charles G. Taylor, leader of the rebel army, who was planning to overthrow President Samuel Doe. "I recall everyone being happy," Simon reflected. "The adults felt their 'savior,' Charles G. Taylor, was coming to free them from what they felt was the dictatorship of President Samuel Doe, but deep down inside I knew something wasn't right. If they knew what was coming, they wouldn't have been as happy as they were. Now everybody knows that Taylor came under false pretenses and created destruction."

Throughout the next few months Simon and his family heard reports that rebel leaders were getting closer to the interior and Doe's troops were fighting back. By April of 1990, his parents in the United States, who weren't allowed to return to Liberia, demanded that Simon and his younger sister leave their older brothers and live with cousins in a neighboring village, which wasn't far. Their older brothers would maintain the house.

There was still chaos in his cousin's area; President Doe was attacking Taylor's rebel leaders with missiles landing in their village. By June, the bombing steadily increased, and his cousins insisted on moving farther north, behind rebel lines. Simon and his younger sister were forced to leave the village entirely. "I left my village with flip-flops, five gallons of palm oil, half a bag of rice, and a lifetime of memories," Simon recalled. He never saw his village or childhood home again.

Simon's older brothers were also forced to flee the village with their grandmother, who they carried in a wheelbarrow because she could not walk due to a stroke. Unfortunately, the neighboring village was not safe, and his brothers knew they had to travel north. "My grandmother didn't have the strength to go. My brothers begged to stay, or carry her, but she demanded they leave. They had no choice and left to get behind rebel lines. They came back a few days later, and the entire village was destroyed. After all this time, no one knows what happened to my grandmother. When the rebels arrived, all they found were dead bodies piled on top of each other. We assumed they had a mass killing and she was killed." Liberians were quickly realizing that Charles G. Taylor and the rebel leaders were not saviors, but were just as corrupt as President Doe.

In the chaos of Simon's brothers returning to their old village, he lost contact with them. He and his older cousins trekked for days to several refugee camps. Simon recalled grueling walks, two weeks at a time, looking for a safe place. There were various checkpoints, filled with rebel soldiers who interrogated every person, and if they weren't satisfied with the answers, people were killed or tortured. Simon reflected, "One time there was a dead body of a young lady who was pregnant, and she was cut from the throat all the way to her vagina with her dead baby lying to the side of her. The rebel was telling someone they were torturing if they didn't tell the truth they'd end up just like her." Shocked by Simon's description, I asked how he handled seeing such brutality at a young age. He casually answered, "By then, everybody had grown up—children are resilient regardless of age. They adapt quickly, so no one had time to process and say, 'This is going to have an emotional scar on me.' It's all about surviving." There was a distant, removed tone in Simon's voice. Violence is scarring, no matter when you process.

Simon and his family, separated and living in various places, traveled to several refugee camps over the next few months. By December of 1990, Simon was extremely ill, malnourished, and at six feet tall weighed a fragile eighty-eight pounds. His older cousin, one of the only adult family members who was with him, insisted that Simon check into the local hospital. However, the hospital had no electricity or running water. Simon described the hospital as "a breeding ground for death." He refused to go, and luckily, his brother, whom he had not seen since April, randomly found him at the refugee camp. He and Simon decided to escape Liberia completely.

Simon and his brother walked toward an area where trains were running. After another two-week trek, he was still sickly and malnourished. His brother thought Simon needed to check into a hospital but, again, Simon refused. "I don't know where that strength came from, but I knew I didn't want to go in that hospital. We were walking and I'd get tired, but my brother would scare me by saying, 'I'm going to leave you!' Somehow I kept walking." Eventually they arrived at a refugee camp in the Ivory Coast. Six months later his sister and other brothers arrived. Their paperwork was processed immediately with the United Nations to approve their refugee status, allowing them to move to America to reunite with their parents after a two-year wait.

Massive civil war continued in Liberia, with incalculable amounts of violence. The war officially "ended" in 1996, but Liberia is still trying to recover from the residuals. President Samuel Doe was captured, tortured, and killed by rebels. Charles G. Taylor was elected president in 1997 and served until 2003, leaving a complicated legacy.

"I was blessed; besides my grandmother, I lost no one. Many people lost all of their relatives and loved ones," Simon said, his eyes slightly blurry, as I lay on his chest

"That's an incredible story, Simon. It should be in a book."

"Maybe you'll write it one day," he laughed, rubbing his eyes. "Got me all emotional. I don't think I've ever told anyone I've dated that story."

"Why not?" I asked.

"I guess no one seemed interested. Most people don't listen." Simon jumped up from the couch, heading to the kitchen to make us Liberian food. I noticed long markings, spreading over his muscular back, like the branches of a tree.

"What are those markings on your back?" I asked.

He turned to face me. "Warrior marks."

"Warrior marks?"

"Yeah, we all have them. You can't always see them."

"Very true," I concurred, reflecting on my own warrior marks.

"You know what else I learned from Liberia?"

"What?"

"I have no fear of trying something new or of change. Change always scared me. Not anymore."

I struggle with change. I do not like surprises; I prefer the predictability of routines. I attempt to be prepared for every moment, but we can't shield ourselves from all the blows. You will take some punches straight to the gut, and in the moment where you can't catch your breath is when you learn the most. I learned this valuable lesson from Donte.

In June 2004, at the age of eighteen, Donte graduated from high school in Missouri as homecoming king and a track athlete. Having earned a scholarship, he accomplished one of his lifetime goals of enrolling at Morehouse College, and began his first semester in September of 2004. Only six weeks into the first semester of his freshman year, Donte discovered a small lump on his neck. "My friends thought it was a spider bite, but the lump felt hard, like something was growing. A few days later I woke up and my neck was enlarged and inflamed."

After a series of tests, the earth-shattering news dropped on Donte's optimistic world—he was diagnosed with Hodgkin's lymphoma, a form of lymphatic cancer, in stage 4, the most advanced stage. Instantly and forever, the reality of Donte's life drastically changed. "I broke down and felt like I was in a world by myself. I wasn't even in college for six weeks and all I could think was, I worked so hard to get to this point, and now I would have to go through all of these tests: chemotherapy, possibly radiation, maybe a bone marrow transplant. All of that was a foreign language to me and it literally felt like the end of the world. I saw myself dying; I didn't see myself beating cancer. I didn't say, 'I'm gonna beat this!' I just said, 'I'm going to die.' I was thinking, *it's over.*"

The next several months were uncharted and petrifying territory for Donte. After countless tests and biopsies, doctors discovered the lump on his neck was a tumor that reached to his lungs. In addition, he had tumors around his arms, beneath his groin, and all throughout his body. In November of 2004, a frightened Donte began chemotherapy treatments. "I didn't know what chemotherapy was; all of it was an unknown world to me. All I could think was, I'm about to become a whole different person. At chemo, I was the youngest person there, I was the only young black guy there—I was so many of the 'only things there,' and it was tough realizing I'm going to have to do this every Friday for the next six to nine months or possibly longer." Donte continued, "The most painful thing to go through was always being sick, tired, throwing up, losing weight, and gaining weight. The chemotherapy kills cancer, but it kills the good stuff—your taste buds, memory cells, and so many different things you take for granted."

Not only is the physicality of cancer intense, but so is the emotionality and stigma that comes with the disease. "Many people are misinformed, especially young black people. Most people associate cancer with smoking or drinking—and I knew people who associated cancer with STDs, and it's not like that. With all the misinformation, I learned not to take it personally." However, for all those who were not informed, there was a collective of others who came together as a solid community for Donte. His old high school organized a fundraiser selling bracelets to raise money for his treatments. "Some days I would say I'm not going to treatment, and the people at the cancer center would call me and say, 'Donte, I don't care if you don't want to go. You have to come get better and tell your story.'"

In April of 2005, Donte received amazing news: His body reacted astoundingly well to the treatments. He was officially in remission; however, he would not be "cancer free" until after five years of remission. Nonetheless, the moment restored a hope that he lost when he was first diagnosed. "Hearing that treatments were over took me back to when I first heard I had cancer. You're crying going in, and you're crying going out. The cancer taught me so much and made me a completely different person. When my friends were going to school, I was going through it in a completely different type of realm. We started school together, and although I didn't finish the year with them, I finished treatment when school was over."

Over ten years later, he is still in remission. "Cancer is a blessing and a curse. I have put so many things in perspective that I wouldn't have imagined before, being so young. I've learned not to take things so seriously. It's okay to breathe. I was so intense about school and other things; I didn't have enough time to really live. Now I realize so many different things are out of my control, because there's nothing worse than hearing your health is at risk. You really learn to appreciate the small things. Nothing is more valuable than a good friendship and a relationship."

Shortly after I interviewed Donte, we began seriously dating. I loved Donte not for his beautiful smile or fiery personality, but for his survival skills. I wanted to survive like him. I wanted to soak up his instincts, get a dose of his courage and an ounce of his gratitude. For every person I have ever loved—friends, family, or boyfriends—I fall in love with their warrior marks. You discover the most about a person after you learn what they've survived.

I remember Donte shirtless. I'd trace my fingers over the thick scars on his chest, the marks from cancer treatments. I wrapped my arms around him, kissing the wounds, and he'd sob. "This is the ugliest part of me."

"No, it's not ugly," I said. "They're your warrior marks."

THE SAVAGE HUNT

AT EIGHTEEN, MY FIRST KISS WITH A TWENTY-TWO-YEAR-OLD man snowballed. Week one he confessed to being in love. Week two he talked of moving in together. Week three he thought we should adopt children. "What did I get myself into?" I questioned. I sat with Nikki, my best friend, on a porch on Thirty-Ninth and Walnut Streets in West Philly, ranting about the craziness of my alleged boyfriend. "I can't do this! He's insane. I don't ever see myself dating again!"

Nikki laughed. Although she was only a year older than me, she endured heartbreak many times over, from men and women. "Baby, let me tell you something," she began. "Whether he's the first or the last person you deal with—when it comes to love, you got a long, hard road ahead of you. It's a savage hunt! And if my friends could hear me now, they'd be saying, 'Go on, Nikki! I know that's right!'" After a month, I ended the so-called relationship. I didn't understand his craziness. He appeared desperate and hungry. I questioned Nikki's advice, telling myself the road to love would not be that difficult for me. *If I claim love, it will come,* I thought. Then, I fell in love for the first time. All of my theories were blown to bits. The savage hunt began.

Unexpectedly, cupid shot me in December of 1995. I was on a double date with a friend who insisted Malik and I would be a perfect match. When I saw him, he barely looked me in the eyes; kept his head down and made no conversation with me. Although he was attractive, with his wide smile, low haircut, and all-American guy looks, my soul wasn't moved. But during the dinner, as we sat at an Irish pub in Center City, Philadelphia, and I munched on chicken fingers and fries, I was suddenly hit with a feeling—one that I've never felt since. A clear thought came to mind as "Let It Flow" by Toni Braxton played in the background. The molecules in the room shifted and I thought, *I'm going to be with Malik.* Within weeks, we were together.

With Malik, I knew nothing about love or how to love. I had just started dating men six months before we met. Plus, in the complicated intersection of blackness and gayness, there was no one to tell me how I was supposed to properly conduct myself in a relationship with a man. LGBT people are socialized years behind heterosexuals; straight people take for granted the freedom of being allowed to openly tell someone—anyone—that you have a crush. Heterosexuals dismiss the importance of a schoolyard romance that doesn't solely exist in your brain. Many LGBT folks don't experience the kind of casual dating that straight people experience in middle school and high school until their late teens or early 20s—and for some, not until their 30s.

Somehow, Malik and I made it work. We learned the arduous lessons of love together. Maybe it was the innocence, I was eighteen and he was twenty. We normalized each other. Malik grew up in a strict, religious household, but when we were together he'd beam, "I know this is not a sin." I met his family, who adored me and I am sure they knew we were a couple. Even the most homophobic of parents can sometimes rethink their judgments when they see their child in love. Homosexuality, which isn't even about sex but rather a connection between people, suddenly goes above the groin for parents who truly love their children. When parents accept, "This is the person who takes care of my child when they are sick. This is the person who is loyal. This is the person who makes my child's eyes light up," it's hard to remain married to hateful convictions—hard, but not impossible.

Malik and I moved in together after six months of dating. We found a two-bedroom apartment in Northeast Philadelphia. The first night in our home was powerful. We were fully moved in, boxes everywhere, spread out on our brand new, king-sized bed, with our fingers intertwined. I felt full as I turned to Malik.

"You look so happy," he remarked.

"I am."

"Why?" he asked, playing with the curls in my hair, one of his favorite hobbies.

I paused, not sure how honest I could be, but this was the man I loved. This wasn't my father. I could let my walls crumble. "There is so much love in this room, it's the closest I've ever felt to God. I feel like God is sitting right here next to us." Malik's brown eyes widened, he squeezed my hand and nodded his head. Any residue I had of believing I was a sinner or burning in a Christian or Islamic hell faded in that moment. The love made me clear.

The love was real, but we were young. Your first love isn't supposed to last. The heartbreak is necessary for you to learn. Within a year, our relationship ended. There was no cheating or fighting. We were rapidly growing, being that we were so young, and our paths did not align. I wanted to move to New York City and he loved Philadelphia. Our time was up and we both knew it, but the pain was still severe. I had never experienced heartbreak before. I was unable to function, wrecked to tears at any second, and propelling through the stages of grief.

I collapsed on the floor of the living room in my brand new apartment in the New York City area. I missed him. I called him but he never called me back. I just wanted to hear his voice. I finally understood why my mother laid up all night crying over a man; why people I knew drank themselves unconscious over heartbreak; why my short-term boyfriend before Malik, whom I never loved, was so desperate to be loved.

My first heartbreak was a wound so severe that I felt like the pain would never pass. In many ways, the sting never really subsided. We never fully recover from the initial heartbreak. When we begin to scab over, someone arrives and slices the wound back open. Cupid is a killer.

My savage hunt officially began. Nikki helped to nurse my broken heart as I did hers. "I feel like my heart is on the hooker stroll!" she would say after another implicit or explicit rejection. I laughed and believed the metaphor was analogous. The search for love is cheapening and the desire for partnership transcends every identity. I've seen the strongest people stripped to raw bones over a broken heart. If you work hard enough, you can progress in your education or career, but no matter how much self-proclaimed "work" you accomplish, the struggle for "the one" is never simple. Think of all the time you've invested in dates, phone calls, sex, conversations, and attempts to receive and give love. Love is work. You want a partner, not a project. Your heart is on the auction block, begging to be chosen. If love is a war, many of us are early casualties. As a soldier of love, I've met many souls along the way—some too petty to remember, others just the same person with a different name. The names change, but their situations are deeply familiar.

Peter was a cloud of doom, otherwise known as the Tragic Gay. He exhaustingly complained how gay men were "fucked up" and how every man cheats. He constantly argued it's impossible for two men to maintain a long-lasting connection. Not surprisingly, Peter attracted the types he complained about. Everyone he met cheated, lied to him, and deceived him. His loneliness and desperation to couple led him to choose people he wouldn't accept under affirming circumstances. He never learned to engage in healthy relationships and, I believe, was unknowingly caught in the Law of Attraction. Sadly, desperation allowed people into his life who weren't worth his time. Peter's dating life was a constant tragedy.

Philip was a Pseudo-Thug who foolishly believed he was a homo success because he mastered so-called masculinity. He was well into his thirties with baggy clothes, hat cocked to the side, and spewed embarrassingly inauthentic 'hood lingo. In reality, he was rocking urban drag, even though he was disgusted by drag queens. A drag queen relishes playing a role. Philip believed the Pseudo-Thug was him, never realizing the drag he adopted was a learned behavior. Philip believed all of his problems would be solved if he could be heterosexual. Periodically, Philip managed to sex up a woman, but he never converted. Inside, Philip was painfully lonely and ashamed; he remedied his loneliness with decadent sex that compensated for all of the ways he hated himself. These are the saddest types because no matter how many times they get their dick sucked and avoid sucking, no matter how many times they are a top and claim they never bottom, their sexuality never changes. As Harold told Michael in Mart Crowley's 1968 play, *Boys in the Band*, "You may one day be able to know a heterosexual life if you want it desperately enough. If you pursue it with the fervor with which you annihilate. But you'll always be homosexual as well. Always, Michael. Always. Until the day you die."

Thaddeus was the Narcissist. He spent more time in the gym than he did at work. He was focused on his appearance rather than his personality. He believed everyone desired him, so he posted half-naked images of himself on social media. The first thing he would say after a long day is how many people tried to hit on him: male, female, elderly, young, cis, or trans. "This girl in the elevator was really staring at me—I know she wanted me to fuck her." "Everybody in the club was looking at me." "I think your best friend was looking at my dick." "Your neighbor bumped into me and tried to feel my ass." When it comes to gay men, Thaddeus dropped jewels like, "I can't be around too many gay men because they all want to have sex with me."

In actuality, it's not that people thought Thaddeus was so beautiful; being attractive is relative. He needed to be validated by strangers and social media; therefore, people perceived him as an easy lay. Fuckable, but not conversational or worth engaging.

Matthew thought he was too fat, too skinny, too old, too short, too tall, too dark, too light, and too much of everything. Telling Matthew, "You look good tonight!" would only end in the response, "I gained five pounds." He was a Low Self-Esteem Good Man. He lost all confidence when walking into a gay club, comparing himself to every muscular man and whining, "I could never get someone like that." He was jealous of other people who he cited as being more attractive than him and he eventually isolated himself in a cocoon of "Nobody wants me." Despite all of the creative and sometimes unique ways in which Matthew hated himself, he would actually be a great boyfriend. This Low Self-Esteem Good Man lived alone and had a career (not just a job), a sense of humor, and intelligence, but he ignored all of these attractive aspects and focused on what he claimed would keep him alone and unhappy forever.

Paul was an Affection Whore. He didn't have sex with every man he met, but he shared a bed, kisses, hugs, and his life story in seventy-two hours. He judged any man who had sex immediately as a tramp; however, he didn't realize that every time he gave away a piece of himself with intimacy, even if he didn't have sex, he was emptier than the promiscuous man, because at least the slut didn't expect anything in return. Paul felt he was doing everything right by waiting before sex and invested all of his time in a man he met less than a week ago. He quickly dived into romantic fantasyland after date one, seeing his whole life play out with his new flame: living together, joint accounts, traveling, and, of course, adopting children. No one could live up to Paul's dream, and once this Affection Whore realized the guy is not what he fantasized, he moved on to the next man and unknowingly had the same experience. All the while, he asserted, "I am not having sex with every guy I meet like everyone else!" Paul never realized there was no formula to make a relationship work, because if there were, most of us would be in relationships. He tried to patch up his toxic issues, but failed when a shiny, new man came along. Maybe it was the love he didn't receive as a child, maybe a relationship broke his heart and he never moved on, or maybe he didn't love himself.

The endgame is to find your match. If you find yourself in one of these categories, or a combination of the categories, it's your responsibility to challenge yourself and change your behavior, to break your pattern. Granted, there's a stigma around being LGBT. However, heterosexual relationships (especially for women) can be just as intense and devastating: children, the pressure of marriage, and prearranged roles that have tortured many for eons. Sometimes we block ourselves by insisting on foolish standards that aren't needs. Like the six-feet-and-taller fetishes, masculine muscular fantasies—you can be tall, masculine, and muscular and be a miserable human being. Do the work to deconstruct these preferences, which are rooted in society's constructed standards that are not your own.

We shouldn't shame people for being single; owning alone time is crucial for developing into better versions of ourselves. I often hear black gay men say, "But I don't see enough successful black gay couples!" Just because you do not see it doesn't mean it doesn't exist. We cannot box ourselves in to what we can see; the key to living a fruitful life is reaching for the things that aren't in plain view. I have seen black gay men in healthy, long-term relationships. The success stories are real. You may not see them in the club; you obviously won't see them on a dating app; but black gay relationships are not a well of deep despair. During the savage hunt, the goal is to be the person and find the person who transcends the categories. Your future Romeo may appear in a package you never expected—imagine that. Now…if only I could take my own advice. Happy hunting!

I AM HIV

ACCORDING TO THE CDC, IN 2010, 28 PERCENT OF ALL BLACK men who had sex with men in the United States were living with HIV, compared with 16 percent of white men who had sex with men[1].

Nearly 3 percent of black gay men were infected with HIV, a rate 50 percent higher than among their white counterparts, according to the CDC in 2012[2].

In 2016, the CDC claimed half of black gay men will eventually contract HIV, the most sobering statistic to date[3].

These numbers haunt me. The statistics are stark, affecting every aspect of life for black gay men: dating, friendships, health care, sex, love, and death. HIV/AIDS is our salient identity, omnipresent and impossible to dismiss. This narrative rarely goes beyond the demonizing numbers, failing to unpack the implications of race, class, and homophobia in a US and global context.

I first heard the term *AIDS* in elementary school. As part of health education, I watched a short film about a young black man (it was implied that he was not hetero) in New York City who was suffering from a mysterious

1 Julie Steenhuysen, "1 in 5 gay, bisexual men in US cities has HIV," Reuters, September 23, 2010, http://www.reuters.com/article/us-aids-usa-idUSTRE68M3H220100923

2 Kenyon Farrow, "Study: 3 Percent of Black Gay Men Become Infected Every Year," Black AIDS Institute, https://www.blackaids.org/news-2012/1305-study-3-percent-of-black-gay-men-become-infected-every-year

3 "Lifetime Risk of HIV Diagnosis," CDC.gov, February 23, 2016, https://www.cdc.gov/nchhstp/newsroom/2016/croi-press-release-risk.html

disease. The imagery was confusing and tragic, causing my first spark of fear. I knew I was gay, and I wondered if the fate of this young man would inevitably be mine. At the movie's end, the man collapsed, lesions covering his body. My elementary-school mind was left with an eerie question: *Is this what happens to all men who have sex with men?*

I didn't get an HIV test until I was twenty years old. Although I was constantly around people who were advocates of safer sex and knowing your status, I, like many others, was terrified. I was afraid of the test, the wait, and the result.

After landing a random job in Philadelphia, I was blessed with health insurance. Excited to have a gig that included benefits, I pulled out the phone book and ignorantly searched for the closest doctor in my area. I had no intention of finally getting tested; I wanted a standard checkup and a prescription to clear up acne.

The moment I saw the doctor I was hesitant. He was an older white man with a stiff manner who barely made eye contact. Yet he appeared comfortable until he peeked at my chart, where I marked my sexual partners as male. After he glanced at me, then glanced back at the chart, I knew he conjured up a pot of assumptions.

Ignoring my intuition, I casually explained my main reason for the appointment was acne and that I needed a prescription. Without responding, he blinded me with a massive surgery lamp, inspecting my face. As he squinted through huge glasses, he spat, "Those are the kind of bumps people who have AIDS get—we better draw blood!"

My mouth went dry. I lost feeling in my fingertips and became dizzy, remembering the video about AIDS from elementary school. Had he just diagnosed me with AIDS? I was a young man who dodged being tested and feared the disease; "AIDS" was all I heard. The doctor pointed me to a doorway where a nurse would draw blood. Other patients, all older white people, sat in the waiting area as the insensitive doctor shouted to the nurse, "HIV testing!" The onlookers stared at me with judgment and pity.

Sensing my fear, the nurse hastily sat me down and asked what was wrong. I told her I was scared. She unsympathetically asked, "You're not going to pass out, are you?" I ignored her as she prepared the needle. She snapped, "Well, if you didn't do anything, you don't have anything to worry about!" She slipped the needle into my arm—I later developed a bruise—and filled two vials with my blood. I left the doctor's office disoriented and angry.

During a hellish weeklong wait, I saw a dermatologist (and got my acne cleared up) and, not trusting the doctor I saw, visited Planned Parenthood for another test. They asked a series of questions about my sexual health, explained safer sex practices, and encouraged me to contact them if I had any questions during the wait. This was the support I needed.

A week later, I called the awful first doctor, who—to my surprise—gave me my results via phone. He flatly stated, "You're fine." I breathed for what felt like the first time in a week.

"You're the most unprofessional doctor I ever had," I began. "How dare you tell me I had AIDS because I had acne? I hope you're never on the other side of the table!" I hung up as he repeatedly yelled, "Wait a minute!" My results from Planned Parenthood were negative as well. I had never participated in condomless sex, but the fear got the best of me.

After that experience, one of my closest friends, James, made it his mission to educate me on HIV/AIDS. Since his teens, he worked in the field of HIV/AIDS prevention and intervention. He empowered my sexuality, removed the shame, and made me promise to "Never be a dumbass again and go to a random doctor in the phone book. You're black and gay. We need specialists, damn it!" James was proud of his advocacy, and shortly after I left Philadelphia in 1998, he moved to Atlanta, Georgia. Years passed, and due to the distance, we grew apart.

In 2008, James said he was visiting Philly and he specifically wanted to see me. "So get your black ass on the ten-dollar Chinatown bus and come to your hometown." A few days later, I rushed down Market Street in Center City, Philadelphia, to see my dear friend. The minute I spotted his car, he hopped out and opened his arms. I was jolted. James was rail-thin; his clothes hung on him as if on a wire hanger. This was not the James I knew. I gave him a hug and could feel his bones; I lifted him up and he was light as paper. "You look good, bitch!" he complimented me with a laugh. Before I could respond, he insisted I get in the car and go back to his "must-see fabulous hotel room."

As we drove to the hotel, I pretended things were like they used to be, but those things were just our past. I was shocked he looked so ill. Regardless of his health status, there was no reason for him to appear so sickly. I knew there was a deeper issue.

When we arrived at the hotel, James continued to babble, cracking jokes and laughing harder than usual. He flopped onto a couch, pulled up a small table, and rolled a blunt. "Sit down and don't judge me for this blunt. I'm sure you're still a prude," he half-joked.

"I'm not judging you, James," I replied, sitting across from him.

James lit the blunt and took a puff. "Well," he began. "I got the HIV." He sarcastically added, "Don't go crying now—I got some Xanax if your ass needs to calm down!" We didn't know each other anymore. He still saw me as the twenty-year-old who was terrified of HIV. I learned lessons from him. My sexuality came with shame that he helped me overcome. Sex did not mean death. My twenty-year-old self felt like many lifetimes ago.

I ignored his sarcasm. "How are you feeling?"

"Oh, I'm great! Yeah, I'm good." He took a longer puff. "I know I'm skinny as all fuck, but I lost weight way before I was positive, got this really fucked-up flu. Then once I tested positive it was hard to gain the weight back." He puffed again. "I started experimenting in sex parties and porn, decided to try that, too. Pill here, snort there. Yeah, the stat is true: If four people are in a room, one of them is sick—that's me!" Big laughs. "Yeah, you know I left you something in my will—but don't get too excited, it wasn't no money!" Big laughs. "Yeah, I'll be working on this porn, but I won't be co-starring in it this time!" Big laughs.

These jokes were harsh and unfunny. I was getting angry, but I understood he was using his version of humor as a coping mechanism. That said, I knew this mask wasn't James. He was one of my best friends, he was my roots. He taught me what it meant to be bold and unapologetic. He helped me affirm myself when no one else would. I wanted to storm out of the hotel, my frustration was rising, but I was afraid if I left I might never see him again. I didn't want this to be our final conversation. So I said what was in my heart: "Cut the bullshit. I'm not one of your dates." He stopped smoking. "You can't tell me everything you just told me and say you're okay. Don't lie to me and expect me to believe it—you taught me better than that."

For just a moment, he slid the mask off, put his guard down, and admitted he had a problem—but he was the problem; not HIV, not drugs, no one else but him. He confessed to letting his ex-boyfriend penetrate him raw, even though he knew his ex—who was now dead—was positive. "Why did you have raw sex with a man you knew was positive?" I gently asked.

James shrugged his shoulders, shook his head, and gave the most honest answer in him. "Maybe if I loved myself, I wouldn't be HIV-positive. I had all the education. I read all the right books. Listened to all the right people.

But it doesn't matter if you don't love yourself enough. That's all I can say." That's all he had to say. Without a foundation of compassion for yourself, no amount of prevention or intervention will save or reinvent you. When I hugged him goodbye, I grabbed onto him like he was my son. I kissed him on the cheek, wondering if this would be the last time I would see him. I knew James could turn it all around. Before I left, I gave him a second hug. "Stop being so damn dramatic!" he laughed, pushing me off.

When I left the hotel I listened to "One Headlight" by the Wallflowers and didn't shed a tear. I rode the train home, soaking in the view of the trees, river, and sky. I played "Home" by Stephanie Mills on loop, but my eyes didn't well up. However, when I finally arrived to my small apartment with no music, no scenery, and nothing to cloud my thoughts, I sat on my bed, thought of the whole day, and cried.

HIV is not only a physical disease; it's also an emotional disease. We live with a unique fear, one that does not cultivate self-love or foster an environment of empowerment for black gay men; traditional tools of prevention, one-size-fits-all PrEP pills, and information about condoms will not lower our rate of HIV/AIDS. Until we learn to navigate the double consciousness of blackness and gayness and arrive at a place where self-acceptance does not depend on external validation from either the black community or the LGBT community, we will be the circus show of the cryptic CDC numbers.

James and my generation lived a different experience with HIV from the era before us. We received all the education, facts, and history. An HIV educator once told me, "There's no reason for any of you to be HIV-positive through unsafe sex, because now you know how to protect yourselves. My generation didn't know." I believed him. The teachers in our community taught us our lives are valuable enough to protect, but the numbers are only increasing. I've relived my story with James many times over, just with different people. Thankfully, James survived and turned his life around, like I knew he could.

RACE

PLANTATION LIFE

THE END OF THE MONTH IS A SIGNAL OF THE APOCALYPSE
when you are living below the poverty line. While my mother did what she
needed to do to put food on the table, she also grabbed extra work wherever
she could find it, no matter how difficult. My mother's best friend Karla, who
was a young Mexican woman with two kids, told her about picking fruit on
berry plantations deep in Washington State. "The work is hell, but it's quick
money and it's under the table. Girl, you're white; I don't think you can
handle it!" Karla half-joked.

"I can handle it when I get that money," my mother declared. "I'll be
there!" For my mom, anything was better than starving.

In 1980s Washington, there was an influx of migrant workers from California, originally from Mexico, searching for work. As Karla explained,
some Mexicans had the impression that there was more work with less
competition, and less hellish heat, in Washington compared to Cali. Many
of these workers lived in the United States illegally; therefore, they took
the jobs no American would consider on their worst day. The labor was
demeaning, with little pay and even less respect. The workers on fruit plantations included a few Native Americans, but were otherwise overwhelm-
ingly Mexican—considered the lowest class of people in Washington State
in the 1980s. Fruit plantations were one of the only places where undocumented workers could land jobs under the table, providing a safe haven for
their "illegal" status. The pay was low, the work long, and the conditions
rough. Washington State is known for its apples, berries, and countless other

fruits, especially during the summer. These were the field jobs you couldn't find in the classifieds.

The work was daily, but our first trip was on a weekend. My mother could never have found a babysitter at four a.m., which was when a dusty blue school bus picked us up on a random, desolate road. She framed the ride as an "adventure," which got me excited. Our first time heading to the berry plantations, the workers were shocked to see a white woman and her black son on the bus. Eyes squinted and jaws dropped. People spoke rapidly in Spanish as we made our way to the back of the bus. "What are they saying, Karla?" my mom asked.

"They're saying in Spanish, 'She better sit at the back of the bus,'" Karla whispered, making my mom laugh. "They're shocked you're here. White people don't do this kind of work, Julie. You know that."

"Well, I don't think I'm too good for any work. I need to feed my kid."

"Yes, and they respect that." The chatter quickly stopped when Karla introduced my mom and me in Spanish to the people closest to us. Word spread during the hour-long bus ride that my mother and I were 1980s poor like the rest of them. Class overrode our American privilege.

The journey through the valleys and plains of Washington was equally beautiful and brutal. The Evergreen State is distinctly green, and viewing the scenery before the sun rose was stunning, with epic trees, gigantic fields, and the scent of summer in the air. However, the bus was packed with people sitting on each other's laps: men, women, and several children. The ride was like sitting in a covered wagon on the Oregon Trail in the 1800s—you felt every bump, shielding your head from smacking against the top of the bus, and the dirt sneaked onto the bus due to the cracked windows. When the hour-long ride finally ended, I never wanted to sit again. Little did I know that feeling would dissipate within an hour.

We arrived bright and early at a desolate plantation that could've easily been the setting for *Roots*. I couldn't take my eyes off the neverending field with rows of berry patches, which confused me. "Where are the berry trees?" I asked.

"Berries grow in bushes," Karla replied.

"Oh," I said with disappointment. I'd imagined I would be hopping around plucking berries from a tree and tossing the delicious fruit into a basket like one of the blonde girls from a Disney movie. There was nothing cartoonish about the berries. The bushes stood like a torture device from a horror film, about three feet tall, surrounded by a fortress of sharp, shiny thorns and thick, lush leaves. I saw more thorns than berries! The creepy sounds of insects were the soundtrack: beetles, spiders, and a flock of bees. *I have to put my hand in there?* I thought.

Now I understood why we were dressed in hats and clothes down to our wrists and ankles, and why my mom lathered me with sunscreen and insect repellent. Plus, snakes slithered through the field, making my mom grip my hand. I thought she would faint as she exclaimed, "Oh my God, there are snakes here!"

"I know," Karla sighed. "They still scare me, but I think of the milk, bread, and butter I can buy at the end of the day."

I squeezed my mom's hand back. "It's okay. I'll protect you." Mom laughed, but the snakes and grimy insects weren't even the worst part of the gig.

Who owned the berry plantations? Take a wild guess. This particular plantation was owned by an elderly white couple who lived in a big, two-story white house, which sat on the side of the plantation with hauntingly huge windows that reminded me of eyes. Someone was always watching to make sure the work was done.

As we workers lined up outside the entrance to the rows of berry bushes, a pale white man with a huge hat explained the schedule while a short, stocky Mexican man with an equally large hat translated coldly in Spanish next to him. "You will make four dollars per crate," he croaked with a shaky voice. The workers immediately started hollering after the translation. Karla explained the rate was five dollars per crate, and he unexpectedly lowered the rate. The white man slowly raised his hands, saying, "I know, I know, but the price of maintenance went up. This is the American way." My mother chuckled, and he quickly shot daggers at her with his eyes. "A thirty-minute break is at nine a.m. and the work day ends at one p.m. As you know, it gets too hot to work past that time, but I'm sure you Mexicans are used to the heat," he said with a giggle. My mother groaned; the translator apparently left that line out.

It was five-thirty a.m. We stood at our row of berries, and a horn blew, which marked the beginning of the horror. The berries were buried in the bushes, which protected them from thorns and insects. Every five minutes or so my mother let out a scream, and I jumped back at the sight of a bug I had never seen or heard of in my science classes. Nonetheless, I dug my small hands into the berry patches, immediately scratching them and staining my fingers with the blackberries. There were an infinite number of berries on each bush, forcing you to kneel, crouch, and twist your back in a billion ways. The other workers, including the children, picked fruit like choreographed dancers, effortlessly, smoothly, and their crates filled at a rapid pace. My mother and I tumbled along as the sun blazed.

To ease the pain, sometimes my mom and Karla would break out into song. No, it wasn't a Negro spiritual, but something strange like a Christmas jingle to take our mind off the heat. The workers laughed at us, but joined in, and we were soon singing "Feliz Navidad." I oddly appreciated the holiday song in the summer because of the camaraderie among the workers; moreover, I was rarely around this many people of color in Washington. Although I clearly wasn't Mexican and didn't speak a lick of Spanish, I blended in. They were brown like me.

I examined the faces of the men, women, and children. Earlier, Karla said everyone was around her and my mother's age, early to mid-twenties, but the workers appeared old. The men's faces were scarred, their brows wrinkled, and hands deeply calloused. The women weren't the glamorous ladies I'd seen on the cover of Karla's Latin magazines; there were no smiles or flowers in their hair. These were women forced into cheap labor at an early age. The children had tiny bodies but old faces. I usually saw kids screaming and running; these children sadly knew their place, quickly taught and captured into the structure of oppression. My ten-year-old mind couldn't process all these thoughts, but as I got older, these resilient, dedicated workers remained in my psyche as I heard the racist arguments over immigration from judgmental critics who would never spend a day on a plantation.

Not too far off in the distance and still visible, an old white woman lounged in her rocking chair on the porch of the big, white house. She sipped a large glass of water, staring into the sun, a slight smile on her face. The contrast between the workers and the owner was horrifically symbolic. The workers, beat down by hard labor, struggling to pick enough fruit to survive the day. On the other side, the old white woman in a quiet glee because she was exploiting the disenfranchised. My soul chilled every time I saw her rocking on the porch.

I picked crazily, knowing each berry meant a possible morsel of food later that day. My mom stressed I could rest at any time. Regardless, the deal was that any parent who brought kids (there were many children working) had to put the kids to work. This wasn't a daycare, so even the kids earned their wages. I tried my best, but my little hands were too wounded by thorns, my body violated by bugs under my shirt. The hot sun tanned my brown face, even with the hat. After three embattled hours, nearly delirious, I passed out in the dirt.

For lunch, the plantation provided scraps, which the owners docked from your pay, but fortunately, my mother and Karla whipped together a lunch of cheese sandwiches and Kool-Aid. Cheese sandwiches never tasted so damn good at nine a.m. Sadly, some of the undocumented workers got their first meal of the day during lunch on the berry plantations.

There were always two managers, one white and one Mexican. They were quick to yell if you weren't picking fast enough or the crates weren't full. They didn't pay much attention to my mother and me, just giving us weird stares. "Don't be ashamed of working hard," she'd tell me. "We're lucky this is our first time doing this. Some people do this all their life and no one appreciates it."

Our first day picking berries was disastrous for us physically. Fingers and hands sliced, stained, and bitten, my mother and I picked as many berries as possible, filling up each massive crate; one crate took over an hour to fill. Yes, an hour's worth of hellish work for only four dollars: the American way. When the horn blew at one p.m., we let out a collective sigh and excitedly brought our crates of berries to be weighed. With one look at our six crates, the Mexican manager went ballistic. "You put the crates on top of each other!" he screamed at my mother. "The berries are smashed! None of this is good!" We stacked six crates on top of each other, which appeared to be the right way to store the berries. There was no tutorial or training period for berry picking.

"I didn't know," my mother explained. "I'm sorry. I thought I did it right. No one told me I was doing it wrong."

"Look!" Lifting one of the crates, he pointed to a thin layer of smashed berries.

"All of those berries aren't smashed," Karla interjected. "Ninety percent of those berries are still good!"

"No! Smashed! Not good! And you picked too slow!" Hearing the ruckus and Karla arguing in Spanish and English, the Mexican workers insisted they pay my mother for all the work she had done. They rallied around her, screaming at him in Spanish, agreeing with Karla that only the top layer of berries smashed.

"They're fucking berries!" Karla yelled. "You can still use them even if some are smashed. We're not talking about a crate of eggs."

"No!" he asserted. "Smashed! You and you," he pointed to my mother and Karla, "banned from here. You ruined all these berries! Don't come back!" The elderly white man stood off to the side, head high, glaring at my mother, forehead pink and deeply wrinkled, shooting looks at Karla, me, and back at my mother. We were not welcomed by the planter elite. We didn't earn a penny for the berries we picked that day.

As we rode the ancient bus back, I was struck by the scent of us workers. The heat and musk of our labor permeated my senses. I stared at my fingers, stained black, like they were dipped in black ink. An older Mexican man next to me laughed at the way I examined my hands, trying to rub the black off on my pants. He reckoned, "You're a real Mexican now."

Fortunately, there were several berry plantations in Washington, and throughout the summer, my mother, Karla, and I, and sometimes Karla's kids, traveled for work. This was short-lived; the work was hell, the hours long, and the exhaustion at the end of the day was debilitating. No one should work under those conditions, but they do, even as you are reading this. Even without the language to express it, my summer on plantations helped me to recognize my own privilege. Being an undocumented worker is a struggle I cannot fathom.

Whenever I hear the term *undocumented workers*, I think of the hardworking, complaint-free, and dedicated people on those berry plantations. They did the work other Washingtonians would never agree to in their worst nightmares and suffered terrible treatment from the plantation owners. When immigration pops up in the news cycle, my small taste of plantation life floods my heart. Whenever I see a blackberry, those sweet, squishy, bumpy pieces of fruit, I remember struggling to help my mom fill her crate with berries so we could earn our four dollars. Every time I pass blackberries in a grocery store, I remember those fields. Blackberries still give me post-traumatic stress syndrome.

TRASH

"YOU FAGGOT NIGGER!" KATIE BARKED, PUSHING ME against a locker, finger in my face. This was my daily hell in seventh grade, I was harassed by my evil peers in middle school. Black, effeminate, and beyond different, I was bullied so aggressively that the victims of bullies actually bullied *me*. They called me Buckwheat from the *Little Rascals*, Lamar Latrelle from *Revenge of the Nerds,* and every explicitly racist and homophobic epithet they could conjure. I was one of few black kids at our school in Vancouver, Washington. My walk, talk, and look were beyond comprehension for someone like Katie, who personally hated me. My classmates had zero understanding that I had a white parent, which I was never bullied for. I was bullied solely for my blackness and gender expression—the identities they could see. Racists and homophobes do not chop up your resumé of identities; they only acknowledge what makes you different from them.

Katie was a privileged prep, with her Keds shoes, Guess jeans, huge Aqua Net–sprayed hair, and loud mouth. She was taller than I was, wide-bodied, and the official monster of the hallways. I strategically planned my routes to each class to avoid her harassment. This particular morning I was rushing, deciding to take the shorter route, and accidentally brushed up against Katie in the hallway. She went ballistic with a smile on her face, enjoying the crowd surrounding her.

I kept my head down, not making eye contact, trying to edge away as she backed me up against a locker. "Look at me, nigger!" she demanded, pushing herself into me. "Are you touching me, fag? Don't touch me, fag!" She pushed her breasts against my right shoulder and, with a quickness, smacked me across the face. Her crowd of evil bandits laughed, including Brett, her sidekick, a scrawny rich boy, who only harassed me when Katie was by his side.

"Hit him again, Katie!" he egged her on. A rage boiled in me; I was about to explode, still feeling the sting of Katie's slap on my face. A millisecond before I was about to go for her throat, Katie was pushed away, crashing against a locker near me. Belinda, the resident "white trash" of the school, who adored me, was now in Katie's face. Belinda was much shorter than Katie, had stringy blonde hair, never wore makeup, consistently donned a black getup, and lived in a trailer park. As small as she was, her presence was intimidating. She always smelled like a pack of cigarettes, had a quick mouth and a hot temper, but only if you pushed her buttons. Belinda hated most things: the teachers, the students, the school, and especially rich girls like Katie.

"Leave him alone!" Belinda roared.

"Why are you standing up for him, Belinda?" Katie cried, trying to fix her hair, which was damaged from the collapse into the locker. "He's a fucking fag!"

"He's not a fag! And why do you care? Why don't you go fingerbang yourself in the bathroom a second time?" Katie was rumored to have gotten caught masturbating in the girls' bathroom.

"That wasn't true!" she yelled as the kids giggled.

"Get away from here and leave him alone," Belinda ordered. Katie looked at me, fixing her hair again. As Brett helped Katie with her bookbag, he turned to me and spat, "Nigger fag." Katie stomped away, with her followers behind her, including Brett.

"Oh my God!" Belinda yelled. "I hate her! Are you okay?"

"Thanks," I murmured, but I wasn't okay.

Belinda shook her head, "I hate rich people. They think they can treat anybody whatever way they want. Fucking bitches!"

Belinda didn't see Katie as a racist or a homophobe; she saw her as a classist, the bane of her so-called white trash existence. We were too young to discuss or understand the homophobia and racism in Katie and the many kids like her. But Belinda was my shero, the sole reason why Katie eventually gave up on bullying me. We were the rejects: We didn't own fancy clothes, didn't live in the ritzy neighborhoods, and never had a chance at being one of the "cool kids." For Belinda, not being a cool kid made us cool kids; it was my own version of a John Hughes movie friendship.

In the summer of 1990, my mother left her first husband, which landed us in a shelter. I was seriously embarrassed and did my best to keep it a secret from the demons at school. If word got out that I was living in the only shelter in Vancouver, Washington, life would be even more hellish. Daily, I walked home from school with Belinda and a group of alleged "bad" kids with their Iron Maiden shirts, Marlboro cigarettes, ripped jeans, leather jackets, and angry attitudes. I also learned more about Belinda's life during these walks. Her mother was a drug addict who constantly rejected her. "My mother doesn't love me, I just got to deal with it," I remember her saying. I asked about her father, which was the only time she ever snapped at me, "Don't ever talk about my father! I fucking hate him." She took a puff from her cigarette. "He's my worst memory." I never mentioned her father again.

I bonded with Belinda and her friends, but I was petrified they would discover my living situation, so I faithfully said my goodbyes a few blocks away from the shelter then turned a corner. One day, as I was entering the front door of the shelter, I heard a holler from across the street: "Hey!" It was Belinda, puffing on her signature cigarette. *Damn, my secret is out,* I thought. She motioned for me to come across the street, I reluctantly walked over.

"You live in that shelter?" she asked, blowing smoke in the air.

"Yeah," I replied with my head down.

She stared past me, heavy black eyeliner etching hazel eyes, appearing to reflect on her own experience. "I used to live there. Saved my life. Then I was sent to juvie for beating this girl up." Belinda took another puff. "Don't worry, I won't tell anyone. I get it." I wasn't sure if I could believe Belinda; there were very few people I trusted in Washington State. "We're not that different," she added, sensing my nervousness. "We're both outsiders. Those rich people are never going to like me and they're never going to like you." Belinda was right, and she never told a soul I lived in that shelter.

In October of 1991, I moved to Philadelphia to live with my father, but I returned to Washington in 1993. I was sixteen years old, over six feet tall, and now a product of the brutal City of Brotherly Love. I was seriously angry and promised myself I would not be bullied again. I arrived at high school with many of the same old demons from middle school. The first day of school, there were whispers all around. I seemed like a different person; I barely spoke to anyone. I trusted no one. Fortunately, I didn't have classes with the main culprits from middle school, except for the last class of the day. All of the horrific faces were there, including Katie, the bully who slapped me, and Brett, her goofy sidekick, who was once taller than me, but his growth had clearly been stunted in the seventh grade. I made eye contact with as many of them as possible as I walked into the class. No more bowed head, no more fear.

Assigned seating forced me to sit behind Katie and Brett, which I knew would be trouble. The moment I sat down, Katie and Brett kept turning their heads toward me and giggling. After they looked back at me three times, I locked eyes with Brett and nearly yelled, "Do you have a problem?" Every neck in the room whipped toward me. The teacher jumped with a piece of chalk in his hand, deeply perplexed.

Brett snickered like we were still in the seventh grade and boomed back, just as loud, "You're still a fag!"

There was no Belinda to hold me back. I quickly wrapped my hand around his neck, bolted from the desk, yanked him out of the chair, and threw him across the room like a bowling ball, making his body slam against a projector. Katie screeched, everyone in the class gasped, and the teacher was speechless. Brett's face was beet red as he tried to catch his breath on the floor. None of the privileged kids in Washington had ever seen this type of violence in their classroom. During my two years in Philly, I saw students and teachers beaten bloody. I was changed; this was now my normal. I charged toward Brett, ready to release all my anger on him from middle school. Out of nowhere, one of the so-called white trash kids I knew from middle school blocked me, wrapping his arms around my shoulders, whispering for me to be calm. "You're the fucking faggot!" I roared. "Look at you! On the fucking floor like a bitch!"

"Get out right now!" the teacher screamed. "Go to the principal's office. You are not allowed back in this class—out!" I was pushed to the door.

Word quickly spread around school that I'd attacked a boy who was smaller than me, and a group of boys planned to beat me up. I didn't care. I thought of West Philadelphia. I was stronger than any of these boys would ever be. When the principal sat me down to explain what happened, I casually said, "He called me a faggot and I planned to whoop his ass. No one is going to call me a faggot." I was kicked out of that high school after two days.

I transferred to another high school where no one knew me. It was a fresh start. Thankfully, I bonded with a multicultural group of friends: black, white, Asian, and Mexican. But the school was suffering from diversity issues. Although we were a small group, we had constant strife with students and teachers. Most of the school feared us, and the white kids who were part of our group experienced the most hatred. They were called nigger-lovers and "wiggas"—white niggers. Their parents hated that they hung out with so many blacks and Mexicans. I landed a girlfriend whose parents viewed me as trouble. I was labeled a "bad boy" who was corrupting their white daughter. Now seventeen, with my sexuality coming to the surface, I thought, *How did I become a bad boy? This is not me.*

There was one lone black boy in my history class, Willie. He was loved by everyone, he played every sport, and the preppy white girls fawned over him. Willie came from money and kept exclusively white friends. The handful of other black kids in the school often called him a sellout, but I liked Willie; I believed he was being himself. One day during class, Willie asked to meet after school to go over an upcoming test. I learned better with others and there was no one else in the class I would study with, so I agreed to meet in the main lobby.

The school was quickly emptying out, and Willie was about ten minutes late when he finally showed up. "Sorry I'm late, dude!" he apologized, gently punching my shoulder like I was one of his jock buddies.

"It's cool. So you wanna go to the cafeteria and go over some stuff? It's empty now."

"Yeah, but walk me to my car, my books are in there." Willie was carrying a huge bookbag over his shoulder. I was perplexed as to why his books weren't on him, but I figured the books he needed were in his car.

"Okay." I walked with Willie, but the closer we got to the entrance to the parking lot, the slower he walked.

"You're a cool guy, man," he said, strangely. "I mean, some people have an issue with you and your friends. I don't, but some people do."

My intuition sparked—something was wrong. My stomach tied in knots, not sure what was happening next. Walking closer to the double doors, through the windows I saw a group of white boys in the back of a pickup truck, clearly looking in our direction. I recognized the boys; they hated my friends, which meant they hated me. There were about five of them and they were ready for something. I stopped walking.

"What are they doing there?"

"Oh, those are just my friends," Willie calmly replied. "They want to talk to you." Willie was trying to set me up.

"I'm out of here," I said, turning around, but Willie grabbed my arm.

"They just want to talk," Willie sternly shot back.

I aggressively pulled his hand off my arm. "Nigga, get off me." I grumbled, keeping my eyes on the white boys in the truck. I could see them, but they couldn't see us. Willie looked at me, speechless.

"Nigger?" he repeated.

"Yeah," I confirmed as I slowly walked away from him, not sure what he might do.

"Only white people call me that," he said, apparently more to himself than to me.

"Well, then you're around the wrong white people." I quickly walked away, running into my group of friends—who all happened to be white, including my girlfriend. In that moment, I was faced with two sets of white people—one set that planned to beat me up with the help of their token black friend, and the other, my true friends in a school struggling with diversity issues. They were labeled "poor white trash," but their exposure to poverty and classism gave them compassion. We both knew the taste of government cheese. We remembered the shame of welfare inspectors examining every corner of our home. Every day we struggled to make our rags fashionable for the brutal politics of high school.

I found pieces of liberation in these unique friendships. They were dismissive of trends, popularity, and acceptance. They reconciled being an outsider as the only space where they would fit. In my adult life, embracing being an outsider would help me soar as a filmmaker, writer, and authentic human being. Granted, we were young people, so there was no competition in the workplace or higher education, but these memories of solidarity resonated with me. They saved me from developing a deep mistrust of whiteness. In reality, I've had more in common, felt more sincerity, and engaged in more nuanced discussions about race with poor whites than with rich, privileged, and sheltered black Americans. I am not arguing class trumps race—there is no comparison—but for my story, class is an equally powerful, relevant, and telling narrative. I couldn't have survived Washington State without the "white trash" of my youth, especially Belinda.

By high school, Belinda dropped out and moved to Nebraska, which was where her family was from. We lost touch, but I heard she got heavily involved in drugs. Recently, I searched for her online and found three heart-breaking mug shots of my childhood friend: face sunken, mouth agape, skin scarred, and eyes devoid of any soul. Belinda, who had a profound impact on my life, was now staring back at me—looking like a corpse. Belinda, and others like her, left an indelible mark on my intersections of race and class. They weren't trash, they were empathetic people who saw the glory in solidarity.

ALTHEA

IT WAS SIX A.M., AND ALTHEA WAS DANCING SLOWLY BEFORE her bedroom mirror, singing every note to Prince's "Insatiable" while massaging Luster's Pink Oil Moisturizer into her shoulder-length bob. My favorite cousin was up extra early because she insisted it took an additional thirty minutes to get her hair "just right."

"Althea," I whined, putting a pillow over my head, regretting having slept at her house for my first day at Overbrook High School in West Philadelphia. My father headed to work at four a.m. each morning. He didn't want me to be a millisecond late for my first day and figured Althea would make sure I was on time. "Do you have to play that Prince song over and over?"

"Yes, I do!" she snapped back, smoothing down her baby hairs. "Besides, it's your first day at a new school. You need to get up and get yourself together. This ain't Washington State no more—you're in Philly!"

Although I visited Philadelphia nearly every summer, I was now living in the City of Brotherly Love. It was October of 1991, I was fourteen years old, and my mother insisted that I move from Washington State to Philadelphia to be around my family. For many years, I resented my mother for shipping me off to Philly, but in retrospect, her motherly instincts were correct. I needed to live in a community with others who resembled me.

My mother, a white woman from Jersey who moved to Washington with her mother in the early 1980s to escape my abusive father, knew she could only teach me but so much about being black in America. I was called "nigger" more than I was called my own name in Washington.

That fall, my fourteen-year-old self was catapulted into blackness—not slang, fashion, or music, but the economic, structural, and historical realities that manifested on every block in West Philly. There were no Denise Huxtables or Steve Urkels. Nineteen ninety-one was the height of the crack epidemic. America's "war on drugs"—a war on brown and black people— and most urban cities across the country were in racial turmoil, which only intensified after the brutal beating of Rodney King was caught on camera in 1992. Truthfully, I was petrified of this crash course in alleged manhood and blackness. Ironically, the complicated lessons I learned about gender and race during my first year at Overbrook High School didn't come from my father, but from my seventeen-year-old cousin, Althea.

She was born and raised in West Philly, an only child like me, and every summer we were more like siblings than cousins. Althea was a senior at Overbrook and a bit of a gangster. She dated drug dealers, walked with more swag than any man, and knew how to throw a right hook like a champ. The stories about Althea were legendary, from taping thumbtacks to her knuckles and pounding the life out of a girl who accused her of sleeping with her boyfriend—which she never did—to beating down boys for inappropriately touching her. Althea was hard like Philly concrete, yet still rooted in her femininity, hence mastering the notes to Prince while perfectly styling her hair. Althea was the first person I knew who defied gender roles.

As a freshman and a transplant, I trusted Althea with every fiber of my clueless being. After she styled her hair in a perfect bob and repeated Prince's "Insatiable" three more times, she insisted on dressing me, despite my protest. "Like I said, this ain't Washington anymore. You can't wear flannels and holey jeans. You got to look sharp." Althea forced me to wear dark jeans, which she ironed with a crease in the front, and a black-and-gold shirt with puffy polka dots that made me look like a rejected backup dancer for Kid 'n Play. Maybe this fashion was hot at the time, but I was not confident.

"Are you sure?" I asked Althea as I gazed into the mirror.

"Yes, I am sure! Now let's get a whole lot of gel in your hair! We gotta get you looking like Al B. Sure!" Althea scooped up a massive handful of Ampro black styling gel, massaging the goo into my hair, flattening down the sides, and twisting my roots slightly until I achieved that always-elusive curly look (I should note: I've now advanced to Eco Styler gel). I examined myself in the mirror again. "You look good, cousin!" she assured me. The look wasn't me, but, to be fair, no look was ever me. I had no agency to be who I was, so my goal was to make my various identities invisible. I prayed my urban drag would solidify my safety at Overbrook High School.

As we rode the bus up Sixtieth Street to school, I felt my nerves vibrating. Althea saw the fear on my face. "I know I'm hard on you, but I'm trying to teach you how to live here. I keep saying this—you ain't in Washington anymore. And where we are going now, this ain't school, this is survival. You gotta be a man! You understand?" she asked. I nodded. "There are three things you need to know about being a black man. One, give firm handshakes. Shake my hand!" I delicately shook her hand. "No! Shake the hand—firm!" Althea shook my hand with the grip of life, nearly cracking my bones.

"That hurts!" I whined.

"Doesn't matter! A man gives firm handshakes! Two, stay quiet, because if you are quiet, they'll think you're crazy and leave you alone." I was chatty, and once I became comfortable with someone, I loved to run my mouth. "And I know you like to talk!" she continued, reading my mind. "But only girls run their mouth and you ain't no girl. Got it?" I nodded again. "And the last thing, and this is important as hell, if someone asks to play craps, don't say you don't know how to play, say, 'I don't roll like that.' Because every black man knows how to play craps and if you can't play craps, you ain't no nigga!"

"What's craps?"

Althea's jaw dropped. "Child, it's gonna be a hell of a road for you!"

Overbrook High School sat on a hill like a medieval castle. All of my schools in Washington were one floor, spread out with a courtyard, grass, and trees. Overbrook was an epic six floors, dominating several blocks with its gray stone and metal gates. Right in front of the school's grand doors I noticed two girls fighting and swinging their arms. "Althea! Those girls are fighting!" I pointed.

"Shut up or you're gonna be fighting! There's a fight every day here!"

I walked into Overbrook, overthinking my clothes, my walk, my hair—the intersections of all my identities. Armed security guards surrounded us, and we were ushered inside as they delivered one-liners like, "Y'all kids better not be bad today!"

Althea walked me to my first class. I stood outside of the classroom as kids strolled in, laughing, yelling, and throwing me the quick side-eye. The room appeared small, but there were so many students inside. "I'm scared," I whispered, fiddling with my polka-dot shirt.

"You're gonna be all right. I promise," Althea insisted. "I know it don't feel that way right now, but you just gotta get through the first day." I nod-ded, my nerves still shaking. Just a week ago I'd been in Washington State, hating the bullying, and now I was on the other side of the country, still feeling like an outsider. "I'll meet you after every class," Althea promised. And she did. That first week, after every class, Althea was there, guarding her little cousin. However, at the beginning of week two, she told me, "You're on your own now. You can't always walk these halls with me. You gotta learn how to be a man."

The first week, my classmates stared, trying to figure me out. I gave firm handshakes, stayed quiet, and always said no to playing craps, but these kids were smart. They saw right through me. By week three, the terror officially began. At first period, there was a note on my desk that read: "CLAY, ARE YOU GAY?" I was stunned as kids turned their heads, looking and laugh-ing. I was hoping no one could see that part of me, and I'd thought with all of Althea's help that I was safe. Uncontrollably, tears flooded my eyes. "Oh my God, he's fucking crying!" One of the boys laughed. I heard a chorus of "He's a sissy! What a bitch! That nigga is gay for real!" The teacher, a thin, older white man, snatched the note from me and read it out loud as the kids laughed harder. "*Clay* and *gay* rhymes!" someone shouted.

The teacher yelled at me, "Who gave this to you?"

"I-I-I don't know," I stuttered

"Well, someone had to give it to you!"

"It was on my desk when I came in."

"No! You know who gave it to you. What? You don't want to upset one of your homies?"

The cackling sounded like a comedy show as someone spat, "He don't have no homies." The teacher tore the note in two, threw it in the trash, and yelled for everyone to shut up.

After school, I vented to Althea. "And what did you do?" she asked as we rode the bus back home.

"Nothing, they were all laughing."

"You gotta stand up for yourself or they're gonna push you around for-ever." I didn't know how to fight back. I wasn't a survivor like Althea; I wasn't as strong. Yet she was right: The teasing became more intense. I was pushed in the hallways, my books stolen, even had the legendary "Kick Me" signs taped to my back. I asked teachers for help and they told me to "just ignore them." How could I ignore people I saw for six hours a day?

I thought if I reinvented myself the bullying would stop. Every day after school, I religiously practiced my masculinity in the bathroom mirror: walking, talking, and sitting. I studied the masculine kids at school, mimicking their movements later at home. If only I could not be a "fag" for six hours, I thought, I would be a man.

The taunting was endless, and there was one particular boy, Manny, who was vicious. He called me a faggot as much as the white kids in Washington called me a nigger. He would jump in my face, puff out his chest, and come close to hitting me until a teacher screamed for him to stop. One day, he was grilling me hard in class, tearing down the way I chewed gum: "Damn, nigga—you even chew gum like a faggot. What the fuck is wrong with you?" (To this day, I never chew gum.)

I stared at him, my insides boiling. I quickly examined his face and noticed he had the most profound, sharp, pointy chin. Loud enough so everyone could hear, I spat, "Shut up, chinny-chinny-bang-bang!" The classroom roared with laughter, throwing papers in the air, falling out of their desks as the teacher, an old white woman, casually flipped through a magazine, ignoring us as usual. In Manny's eyes, I saw a slight crack in his facade—I had pushed a button. Quickly that crack turned to anger; he popped up from his desk. "Fuck you, nigga! Come on, boy!" he yelled.

"Calm down, Manny!" the teacher yelled. "Calm down or I'm getting security and you'll be thrown out of school again!" I was proud that I fought back with my words, but little did I know I'd started a war.

Within days, every ninth-grader wanted my ass whooped. Manny told all of the boys that I was looking at him in the locker room during gym class. Manny's girlfriend, Sheena, who was the Queen Bee of the ninth grade, ruled my sixth-period class and made it her daily routine to harass me. She was tall and thick for her age, with her hair in a tight ponytail, and always wore gold hoop earrings. She remains one of the meanest people I've ever met. While I know she was just a child and I was unaware of what her story was at home, this girl cursed me out, spit on me, threatened me, and lived the embodiment of cruelty every day of the ninth grade. After I called her boyfriend "chinny-chinny-bang-bang," I would get notes from her saying, "We beating that ass today, sissy." "Fuck you, fag." "You gonna die after school, bitch."

The Thursday before winter break, I was told by several students that the next day, Friday, was when the violent ass-whooping would go down. I confessed to Althea and my entire family. My father was disappointed that I was "allowing" myself to be bullied. Althea's mother, my Aunt Goldie, said, "Baby, if anyone puts their hands on you, you beat their ass!" I remember thinking to myself, *How the hell am I gonna do that? Do I look like Action Jackson?*

Althea stayed quiet and didn't say a word until we arrived at school that Friday. She walked me to class, the first time since my first week. She glared at me as students sucked their teeth while they walked by. "I guess I'm not much of a man," I said with disappointment, lowering my head in defeat.

"You gotta be who you are. I'll see you after school." I hoped I would make it to sixth period, but at any moment, I could be pulled into a hallway and get the life beaten out of me. Manny wasn't at school that day, but rumor had it he was coming after school—just for me.

In sixth period, evil Sheena paid close attention to me. She passed me a note that read, "Today's the day, fag." I couldn't concentrate. Why were they so cruel to me? Head in my hands, with the useless teacher babbling, I considered leaving early to avoid the inevitable beatdown.

As I was obsessing over my fate, the classroom door slowly creaked open, so loudly that everyone, including the teacher, looked in the direction of the door. There was my cousin Althea, stone-faced, her short frame standing tall, gold jewelry around her neck, brass knuckles on her fingers, and hair in that perfect bob. I never heard the class so silent.

Althea turned to me. "Where's Sheena?" she asked coldly. I quickly pointed her out. Althea stomped over to Sheena, who, for the first time ever, had fear in her eyes. "Let me tell you something, little girl—don't you or your boyfriend put your hands on my cousin." Althea's voice quickly escalated to a yell. "You touch him and I'll fuck you up! You understand me? I will kill you, bitch—don't fuck with me!" The silence was thick. All eyes were on Sheena; even the helpless teacher waited for her response. Althea was ready, fist balled and mouth tight. Although Althea was a senior, Sheena was bigger, but the bully didn't move from her desk. Evil Sheena put her hands up. "I got it. It's cool, no one's gonna touch him."

Althea took a step back, "And that goes for all of you! You say what you want, but don't nobody put your hands on him! Nobody!" she roared. Althea gave another glare at Sheena and walked out. The unfazed teacher returned to his alleged teaching.

After class, I met Althea and two seniors who were built like football players. "Anybody touch you?" Althea asked.

"Nope!"

"And they wouldn't—not after Althea jumped in there, scaring them freshmen," one of her friends said with a laugh. "You a little soft, but you gonna hang with us now," he added, as he put his arm around my shoulder. "Fuck them young kids!"

"I might've put too much pressure on you," Althea said as we walked out of Overbrook.

"Yeah, he's just a young blood!" the other friend added.

"I know, it's just that you're gonna see a lot here in Philly. This city ain't no joke. I need you to be smart, aware. But you really gotta be yourself." The bullying stopped only because my cousin was by my side. She grabbed the leadership role, and built an alliance for me among her crew.

There was no manifest victory that freshman year at Overbrook. I never learned how to be a tough black man from my favorite cousin. However, in her seventeen-year-old way, before terms like *gender nonconforming* and *cisgender* existed, she strangled every notion of "boy" and "girl" roles in my fourteen-year-old brain by simply being herself. When I stepped into my authentic self as a gay man, four years later, I reflected on the three tips for being a black man that Althea gave me on that bus ride to Overbrook. Giving firm handshakes was not about manhood, but about confidence in your introduction to someone. Staying quiet wasn't about people thinking you're crazy, but about listening and observing. You can't hear if you are always demanding to be heard. Never admitting you don't know how to play craps wasn't about proving you're a "nigga," but about knowing how to code switch, even if you don't know the game.

I own my confidence. I take time to listen and observe. Most importantly, I've never lost a game of craps.

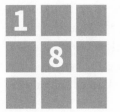

THE WHOLE TOWN'S
LAUGHING AT ME

THE FIRST BROKEN HEARTS I KNEW: MY MOTHER AND MY Aunt Goldie. These two women caused me to reimagine how I viewed pain and, more specifically, black girl pain. Even in the fundamentals of a broken heart, there is no escaping race, class, and gender. In many ways, my mother and Aunt Goldie were alike. I saw each of them in the other, but there were striking differences: my mother white, my Aunt Goldie black; my mother living on the West Coast, my Aunt Goldie living on the East Coast. When I was a child and teenager, their stories confused me. They were similar, but the end results of their stories were dramatically different.

I heard Janis Joplin's voice echoing from my mother's bedroom as I turned the key to our apartment. I knew what Janis meant. Another man had taken a piece of my mother's heart. My insides tensed up as I walked closer to her room; I could hear her sobbing over Janis's savage voice. A mother's tears rips a child open.

Whenever my mother played Janis Joplin, she sank so deep, her body lay on the ocean floor of heartache. The blues singer was my mother's soundtrack to sorrow. When she didn't understand why she had been rejected, when she had given all that was in her spirit and failed, Janis spoke to her. At that time, I couldn't comprehend this well of sadness. My mother was beautiful, strong, kind, and loyal, but she continued to meet the devil in every man she loved.

Her first marriage ended. Although Randy cheated, couldn't keep a job, and caused my mother's already damaged self-esteem to plummet, in her mind, he was an upgrade. "Well, at least he doesn't hit me. He's nice to me," she would explain.

When Randy and my mother separated we ended up in a shelter and eventually a tiny apartment. She felt like a failure as a wife, mother, and woman. She was taught that without a man her life was a failure, even if the man was a failure.

As I tapped on my mother's bedroom door, I shuddered to think of the condition I would find her in. I cracked the door open. "Mom?" I could smell the Budweiser and Marlboro cigarettes in the small bedroom. I locked eyes with her and instantly knew she was drunk, lying on her side, hair disheveled, eyes bloodshot and heavy. "Are you okay?" I asked. She slowly shook her head no. "Can I do anything?"

"I'm sorry you have to see your mother like this," she slurred. Janis Joplin screeched through "A Woman Left Lonely," an eerie backdrop to my mother's wounded heart. Her shaking hand grabbed a burning cigarette from the ashtray. She took a puff. "Here I am again. I just don't know what I'm doing wrong." My mother ran her fingers through her hair as the tears poured out of her. "I can't take getting my heart broken like this. It's killing me. I'm not as strong as I used to be."

My mother was in her early thirties. The weight of many turbulent years had taken its toll on her soul. Once upon a time, she could snap back from any heartbreak, any drug, and any drink. My mother hadn't lived a privileged life; she was in foster care at eleven years old, on the streets as a teenager, and a single mother at eighteen. She was forced to be an adult too young.

"I thought this one would work," she said.

"I know...but you do so much better on your own," I replied, sitting next to her.

"Just me and you, right?" She laughed, patting my hand.

"That's right." I wiped her tears away, gently moving stray hairs off her face.

"You're a good son," she said with a crack in her voice, crying harder.

"And you're a good mom." I was always stunned that a woman could raise and affirm a young black gay boy, but never found the strength to value herself.

"I just don't know any better," my mom conceded. "You know what my mom used to tell me? If I want to keep a man, I should iron his pillow-cases and underwear. That was the dumbest shit I ever heard, but that's what women are taught." She paused. "Baby, I need help. I got to get help. This is more than a man."

My mother found help and discovered that her issues with men were not about her partners, but her mental health. She was clinically depressed. Starting in her early thirties, my mother began a journey of healing. The road was arduous, but, fortunately, and despite living in poverty, she had unlimited support in Washington State. There was always a sponsor, discounts for medications, counselors, and a system to help her find balance no matter how many times she repeated mistakes. I was consistently grateful for the number of chances my mother was given. She'd crash, but, through a network of support, she always found her way back. Even in the early 1990s, when mental health was still a taboo conversation, my mother was granted useful tools that saved her life. The system did not fail my mother in her adult life.

The system in Philadelphia was seriously fractured, which was obvious in my Aunt Goldie who grappled with nearly identical issues to my mother. After I moved to Philadelphia to live with my father at fourteen, I felt incredibly alone and uncomfortable around the aggressive energy of the men in my family. Aunt Goldie was my mother figure. She understood that I was sensitive, still adjusting to the brutality of 1990s Philadelphia, and her home became my refuge from my father. We'd spend hours in her bedroom, listening to the soulful music of her era.

Goldie adored her music. Her love of soul reminded me of my mom. It became a ritual for the two of us to spend a couple hours a week singing along to Diana Ross's *The Boss*, Luther Vandross's *Never Too Much*, and of course, all things Teddy Pendergrass.

"Now this is what you call singing! Teddy!" Goldie would say, putting her hand in the air, moving to the music. His rough, sensual voice never failed to captivate me, and I loved to see my aunt's reaction to her favorite singer. Like my mom, Goldie loved a heartbreaking ballad. Whenever she could relate to the torch songs, Goldie's refuge morphed into a space of dangerous isolation, resulting in weeklong drinking binges that would scare my entire family.

Goldie was in her thirties, a single mother living in West Philadelphia, and, like most women I knew, lived horror stories with the men in her life. I heard the tales of a younger Goldie ferociously beaten up by the father of her child: smacked, kicked, and punched in the face—in public. Goldie also struggled with her weight, suffered from low self-esteem, and, sadly, often gravitated to married men. People in the neighborhood would gossip: "Goldie always wants what she can't have." Who knew what consistently made Goldie crave love that couldn't be reciprocated. However, she didn't exist in an era or community where her afflictions could be analyzed or treated.

A picture of heartbreak, I will never forget Goldie listening to "The Whole Town's Laughing at Me" by Philly soul singer Teddy Pendergrass. This was clearly a day of rejection, as Goldie lay in her queen-size bed, wearing a nightgown on a Saturday afternoon with a bottle of E&J brandy in one hand. Her soul buried itself in the tragedy of the ballad about a love lost. I had never seen my Aunt Goldie this low; usually her binges came with isolation, but I'd randomly popped up for one of our music sessions. By listening to grown folks gossiping, I learned Goldie met a new man who was about to divorce his wife, but this was a script she'd heard before. That said, Goldie loved this man and often talked about him, even while people whispered, "There she goes again with another married man."

"I love Teddy Pendergrass," Goldie said, clumsily placing the needle of her record player to the beginning of "The Whole Town's Laughing at Me."

"But this song makes you so sad, Aunt Goldie."

"No, baby. It makes me feel. Sometimes you get hurt so much you can't feel no more. You need something to make you feel." She turned her head toward me, locking eyes. "I hope he calls," Goldie said as Teddy continued to roar. She stared into a place I couldn't see, taking another swig. "Maybe I said something wrong. One time, he told me I was weak. I'm not weak; I am a strong woman. A strong black woman." Her eyes welled with tears, embarrassment, and repressed anger. The wounds etched in the lines of Goldie's face, the swelling of her eyes, the fidgeting of her hands, and the weight in her voice were palpable. "I'm trying to be strong," she explained, appearing to forget I was in the room. "I can't be strong for everyone." Goldie let out a deep sigh. "I need help." The word "help" rang in my teenage ears. I flashed back to my mother in her bed, acknowledging she needed help. My mother couldn't heal herself on her own; she wasn't a magician, and neither was Goldie.

I thought of the help my mother received in Washington State. These were both women who loved and lost, who made mistakes, who dealt with complex issues that traveled far beyond men. There has got to be similar help in Philadelphia, I thought.

"Can't you get help? Counselors?" I asked Goldie.

Goldie giggled slightly. "What's that? There are no counselors in West Philly. No, I'm strong. I can get better on my own. I always have. I always will. I'm strong. Women like me are built to survive."

While no one could cry like my mother could cry, as a white woman, she wasn't dealt the complex hand of black womanhood. Yes, my mother's pain was just as real and profound, but a black woman's heartache is carved in the narrative that you don't deserve happiness. Your grief is rooted not simply in the desire to be loved as a woman, but in the desire to be loved as a black woman. You are always the pillar of strength, "holding down your man" at any cost.

White women aren't expected to lift up communities. Unlike my mother, who had clearly suffered similar abuse, Goldie struggled under the weight of being "strong," not only for herself, but for every living thing around her. Goldie was forced to strive for the mythical goal of the black woman super-hero. Any expression of rightful rage or wild anger and she'd become the stereotypical angry black woman. Any peep of asking for or seeking help and she would be rendered weak. These were the days before *depression* and *chemical imbalance* were acceptable words, especially for women of color. Goldie, and women like her, were forced to manage without the proper tools to heal. She wasn't given the agency to feel pain. Goldie in her bed listening to Teddy Pendergrass, waiting for a man with a bottle in her hand, was forever branded in my brain.

For years, my Aunt Goldie would lose herself in weeklong drinking binges. She'd unplug her phone, refuse to answer her door, and would take days off work. She'd eventually return from her binges, powerful as ever, ready to battle the world and appear invincible—striving to be the superhero. I thought Goldie, like my mother, was the strongest woman I knew. Also like my mother, Goldie required treatment beyond an emotional patch-up job. For my mother, it wasn't until her fifties that she finally stopped drinking, refused to allow abusive people into her life, and found a regimen of medication that sustained her mental health. Survival is not a solitary experience; it requires a community to lift the wounded.

In January of 1998, my father called early in the morning and told me Goldie passed away at forty-four years old. During another drinking binge, she'd suffered an asthma attack and died alone in her bedroom. As my father reminisced about his sister, years of Goldie flashed through my mind. Memories danced as I thought of the hours we spent in her room listening to the deep soul music of her era. The melody to Teddy Pendergrass's "The Whole Town's Laughing at Me," echoed in my heart. I cried for my Aunt Goldie, lacking the words to verbalize what I was feeling. Goldie didn't die from a broken heart, drinking, or even an asthma attack. The system failed my aunt and continues to fail countless black women. I am eternally grateful my mother is still here. I only wish my Aunt Goldie had been offered an equal set of resources. For Goldie, there was no access to the mental health services that saved my mother. There was no outlet to unpack the clinical intersections of black womanhood. The solution was to be a superwoman. Not everyone can be resilient, not everyone can embody "black girl magic," and even superheroes need a safety net.

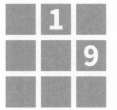

YOUR
AMERICAN LIFE

THERE ARE NO GREATER SYMBOLS OF AMERICAN POVERTY than food stamps, government cheese, and roaches. I've lived with all three.

When I was growing up, food stamps were deeply shameful and looked nothing like actual cash. The embarrassing sixty-dollar food stamp pack was colored a pale orange. There wasn't even a president on the front, just a cracked Liberty Bell. I would beg my mother to rip the food stamps out of the pack and at least place them in her purse to create the illusion of real money. When she handed a cashier the food stamps, I'd cringe at the bright purple five-dollar food stamp with Thomas Jefferson staring with disappointment, lips pursed, as if he were saying, "Shiftless freeloader!"

I'd whine when my mother forced me to go to the store on my own with the food stamps. I was never exactly clear what was and wasn't allowed on food stamps, so I prayed to not be embarrassed in line. I never made eye contact, and my fingers shook slightly as I gave the cashier the food stamps, feeling the heat of eyes on me from other customers in line. The cashier would say, "This! This! And this! Can't buy those on food stamps!"

"Okay," I mumbled, grabbing my bags and blushing as I heard the snickers while I rushed out of the store. Now I see people use the Electronic Benefits Transfer card, which is less humiliating. At least you can swipe at an angle to make it look like a credit card and hope the person behind you won't stereotype you as a lazy welfare recipient.

The days of standing in line for government cheese are history, but back in the 1980s, if you wanted that legendary government cheese, you waited in lengthy lines for a hard block of bright yellow dairy with lethal amounts of food coloring. I despised those waits. I'd lean into my mother, attempting to hide my face, as cars drove by, their occupants staring down at the poor people. My mother knew how much I despised the government cheese line, but she told me, "Never be ashamed to ask for help, especially when there are no jobs—and the jobs you get won't even let you survive." Welfare is a debasing experience. Contrary to the narrative from Republicans like Ronald Reagan, who originated the clueless myth of the "Welfare Queen," we weren't buying steak and lobster. We were coping with the lie of "trickle-down economics." On a somewhat optimistic note, though, 1980s government cheese is still the best cheese I've ever tasted. There was nothing better than a grilled cheese sandwich with the original government cheese. *Way* better than Kraft.

Food stamps and government cheese come with their shame, but roaches—those brown, everlasting, resilient critters—represent one of the most despicable levels of poverty. Not in a place like New York City where you'll find a handful of roaches in luxury high-rises. I am talking about turning on a kitchen light and viewing the raw terror of roaches scattering across the floor, ceiling, and walls. Finding a half-dead roach in a glass of cherry Kool-Aid, scarring your childhood. Being terrified to open a cabinet for fear of a riot of roaches attacking your little fingers. No matter how aggressively you clean, they never leave. Roaches are always there to remind you of your poverty. I once said, "I'll know I've made it in life when I live in a home that doesn't have roaches."

In the ninth grade, I was obsessed with a girl named Karyn who was in my first-period class. She was short and thick, and strutted down the hallways like a warrior goddess. Karyn rocked a motionless mushroom permed bob and wore Christian-conservative clothing that her mother forced on her. By the time she made it to first period, three layers of clothing were stuffed in her bag, her skirt hiked up, and she was poured into a colorful, tight T-shirt, ass cheeks practically out and bosoms jiggling. If I saw Karyn today, I would be mortified and probably pull her to the side to demand she get counseling, but as a young fourteen-year-old gay boy, I saw her as the saucy minx at our school and the closest spectacle to a drag queen—I was a fan.

The other girls violently bullied Karyn. Every other day she was swinging her fists like a windmill at the latest girl who'd pushed her buttons. A handful of the meanest girls called her "Roach Bitch," because at least once

a week, roaches crawled out of her bookbag and scurried across the classroom floor. I would catch Karyn kicking the roaches in the direction of the
front of the class, but I never said a word because I didn't want to embar-
rass her. Like clockwork, the girls (and boys) would scream and fall on top
of each other as the teacher hollered for everyone to calm down. During
the drama, the mean girls would yell, "Roach Bitch! Roach Bitch! Roach
Bitch!" Karyn would sit in the back, unbothered as she applied makeup or
played with her hair.

I adored Karyn, laughed at her jokes, sat in the back of the class with her,
complimented her clothes, and didn't mind if she peeked at my answers during a test. One morning, after about five roaches crawled out of her bag and
the mean girls went on another "Roach Bitch" diatribe, I asked in my nicest
voice, "Karyn, why do roaches come out of your bag? We all have roaches,
but damn!" Karyn giggled, pulled out a small mirror and a tube of hot red
lipstick, and slowly began applying.

"How does this lipstick look?" she asked, puckering at me.

"Perfect," I quickly responded.

"Boy, I have so many roaches that I have to shake the roaches off my
panties when I pull them out of the drawer!" she said with laughter. I envisioned little roaches clinging for dear life onto Karyn's panties as they fell
back into the drawer so that their vile, insect bodies could grip onto another
undergarment. I never looked at her panties the same way again, especially
considering the whole class could get a glimpse once or twice a day with her
revealing clothing.

"Why don't you shake out your bag, though?" I asked. Karyn cut me a
look; I was worried I'd offended her.

"You want the truth?" she whispered. I nodded yes. "You can't tell
nobody." I nodded again.

"Well, every single morning when I get up, I take about five roaches and
put them in a little plastic bag and bring them here to this class. That's why I
sit in the back of the class."

"Huh? Why?"

"So I can drop the roaches out of the plastic bag and nobody sees me.
See, the first time the roaches came out of my backpack was an accident, but
when they wouldn't stop calling me Roach Bitch, I decided I'm gonna be
that Roach Bitch. Now I love seeing those bitches act crazy. One day, I'm
gonna throw a bunch of roaches right at them—especially at one of them

light-skinned girls who keeps calling me that. You watch." Karyn was offi-cially my Dominique Deveraux of the ninth grade.

About a week after Karyn made her confession, roaches crawled out of her bag again, the students screamed on cue, and the girls yelled, "Roach Bitch!" Karyn remained calm, playing with her hair, but this time the teacher lost it. "Karyn! This is happening every week. You have to get this under control. I'm sending you to the principal's office!" The students cheered, except for me, as Karyn slowly gathered her items. "Hurry up, Karyn!" the teacher ordered.

"I am," she replied coolly. With her back turned to the teacher, I saw Karyn pull out a small plastic bag of dead roaches. She gave me a wink and slowly sashayed to the front of the class. Holding the plastic bag behind her back in one hand, she took her time passing one of the light-skinned girls, who stupidly mumbled, "Roach Bitch." With a quickness, Karyn dumped the plastic bag of roaches over the light-skinned girl's head, then ran out of the classroom. The light-skinned girl screeched from her core, smacking her head, then collapsed to the floor and rolled around endlessly, knocking over desks. The entire class joined in screaming and jumped up on their chairs as I sat in the back laughing with tears in my eyes. Karyn was kicked out of the class, but she is branded in my mind as someone who took the most disturb-ing element of poverty and used it as a weapon against bullying. She wasn't Roach Bitch, she was the Baddest Bitch.

I was fifteen and it was a blazing hot afternoon in Philly. I begged my father to drop me off at a friend's house for a barbecue—there is nothing better than a barbecue in the city on a steamy summer day. I was starved and in the mood for some potato salad, ribs, mac and cheese, and everything else on the unhealthy soul-food diet. The minute I arrived, everybody happily ordered me to go into the kitchen and get a plate. I peered into the kitchen from the backyard and saw plates, bowls, and aluminum pans filled with food. *Hot damn!* I thought. With "Superstitious" by Stevie Wonder blasting through the backyard and house, I made my way to the kitchen.

I couldn't move. I could barely breathe. The vision before me was para-lyzing. Roaches were colonizing the kitchen: the tables, floor, and walls. Although all of the food was secure with an aluminum foil covering or a lid, my teenage self was still disturbed. A woman rushed by me, scooped up a plate of food, shook a roach off her hand, and dashed back out. "Oh, hell no!"

I said to myself. Anyone who has attended a black family barbecue knows the cardinal sin is not eating, which is highly disrespectful and unforgivable. In my teenage mind, I found it categorically necessary to take a revolutionary stand and not eat at the barbecue. I inched my way to the backyard, where everyone asked me why I wasn't eating. I lied and said I was feeling woozy. They could smell the bullshit and gave me the serious side-eye with a "Hmph!" I called my father and begged him to pick me up; he took hours to arrive while everyone at the barbecue judged me. When my father finally showed up, he proceeded to cuss me out for being spoiled, ungrateful, and childish, but I didn't care. I just knew one of those roaches was baked into the mac and cheese. Roaches at a barbecue are disturbing, but of course, in retrospect, what were they supposed to do? Not barbecue? Not cook? In poverty, you work with what you have, and all they had was a house with an infestation.

Being that I've been socialized and raised with those damn bugs, I still live like I have roaches. I rinse off all dishware before using it. When I throw little scraps of food in the garbage, I wrap it in a plastic bag first. I take out my garbage once, maybe twice a day. I never leave food sitting on the stove. I wash my dishes immediately. The list doesn't stop.

Roaches are deep manifestations of poverty. Yes, they're hilarious at times, but those critters still come with embarrassment. Roaches are welfare checks, government cheese, food stamps, and section 8 all come to life as a living, breathing, multiplying being. For poor people, one of the greatest efforts in the midst of economic squalor is to be "clean." Roaches remind you, no matter how immaculate you strive to be, this is the gutter, this is your life.

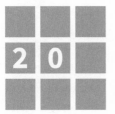 # TRAGIC MULATTO

THE SUMMER OF 1986 WAS MY FIRST TIME FLYING. I WAS terrified as my mother walked me to my aisle seat in the non-smoking section of a Continental Airlines airplane (these were the days before intense security checks and, yes, people even smoked in flight—I vividly remember ashtrays in the chairs). My mother hugged me tightly as I started to cry and asked her, "Can't you come with me?" This would be my first time away from my mother for this long. One month in Philadelphia with my father.

"No, baby," she responded. "You need this trip. You need to be around your father and your family...and Philly." I didn't understand what she meant at that time, but my mother wanted me around other black people. Although we had only been on the West Coast for about five years, all of my memories began in Washington State. I already heard "nigger" more times than I could remember. I experienced racism in and out of school, from students and neighbors. Undoubtedly, Washington had superb public education and Philly was ravaged by the crack epidemic, but I was missing the education of black-ness. Although my mother was white, I was never perceived as white, which my mother understood. She knew, and I knew, I was black. Not a biracial mixed combo. This was the reality of my experience.

When I arrived in Philadelphia, my entire family met me. There was my father, arms open as I walked through the corridor. He scooped me up and introduced me to my cousins, aunts, and grandfather. All people my mother told me so much about over the years. *Everyone looks like me,* I remember thinking. "Nigger" was branded in my brain, in Washington State, I was the lone brown face for miles. Here, at the Philadelphia airport in 1986, was my first positive and affirming realization of melanin, a lesson my mother was unable to fully teach me in Washington.

By 1991, I was fourteen and officially living in the City of Brotherly Love with my father. For all of the mistakes my father made, I can own that he, along with my mother, ensured I wasn't a stereotypical tragic mulatto. Neither of them taught me I was "special" because my mother was white and my father was black. My parents never praised me with asinine terms like "good hair," a phrase in the black American community that's wrongly used to praise hair that isn't "kinky." I can't recall hearing "light-skinned" in my house. Whether I was living with my mother or father, there was no talk of being "mixed." In white neighborhoods in Washington State, no one questioned my racial identity. One child labeled me "Buckwheat" from the *Little Rascals* because I was the darkest person he'd seen. In black neighborhoods in Philadelphia, I wasn't a light-skinned rarity. Blackness is every hue and texture.

Yes, I struggled with identity issues, not as a result of having parents of different races, but as a result of being a minority in America. That said, when I was growing up, the majority of black Americans in the media resembled me, a clear example of colorism. When I hear so-called "mixed" people gushing about early Mariah Carey by saying, "She was the first person I saw who looked like me!" I think, *What planet were you living on?* For decades, lighter-skinned black Americans were the main representation of blackness, especially in the 1980s: Jasmine Guy, Lisa Bonet, Prince, Al B. Sure, Rae Dawn Chong, Denise "Vanity" Matthews, El DeBarge, and, eventually, Michael Jackson. But in my home, I was never valorized for being "mixed." Today, I am secure in my identity because my parents taught me to own the reality of my blackness.

In November of 2015, Taye Diggs reignited a controversial and difficult conversation: racial identity. The actor talked to theGrio.com about his fears that his son, Walker, would be labeled as black. He explained, "When you [call biracial kids Black], you risk disrespecting that one half of who you are and that's my fear. I don't want my son to be in a situation where he calls himself Black and everyone thinks he has a black mom and a black dad, and then they see a white mother, they wonder, 'Oh, what's going on?'" Taye also released a children's book titled *Mixed Me*.

Taye Diggs's strange terror that people will perceive his son as black negates the legacy of countless black Americans with white parents. Contrary to Taye's theory, my white mother was mortified by the idea that I wouldn't recognize myself as black. A white woman who didn't even finish high school possessed the emotional intelligence to understand that I needed to be prepared for racism in school, my neighborhood, and, God forbid, the criminal justice system. My mother didn't want me to live in a world of delusion. By owning blackness, I was never denying her or my background. I simply accepted my reality.

Taye Diggs is a striking contrast to my black father, who bluntly explained, "You're seen as black. I need you to know that when you leave this house. You're a black man in America." Maybe this is a class issue. Taye's son will grow up in an excess of luxury with his actor father and Broadway star of a mother, Idina Menzel. More than likely, he will never grapple with the racism I endured from the trailer parks of Washington State to the ghetto of West Philadelphia. Taye's son is starting life with grand privilege.

Juxtapose Diggs's comments with Halle Berry's five years earlier; the conversation is wildly different. In 2011, *Ebony* magazine asked if her daughter, Nahla, was black American, and the Oscar-winning actress answered, "I feel like she's black. I'm black and I'm her mother, and I believe in the one-drop theory." Just like with Taye in 2015, bloggers raged, and suddenly everyone was an expert on dissecting the social construction of race. It was as if a chapter from an Alex Haley book had come to life on the Web.

Berry, who has a white mother and black father, never used the words "mixed" or "biracial" to describe her racial identity. She identifies as black. Similarly, President Barack Obama, Faith Evans, and even the late, great Bob Marley all embraced having a white parent—but didn't identify by degrees of blackness. In 2017, this mindset is rapidly changing; many want to be "multi." People proudly run through their races, ethnicities, and nationalities as if they're a resumé. "Mixed," "multiethnic," and even the deeply offensive word "mulatto" are resurging as the hottest labels.

The stretch to identify as "mixed" is a compulsory social step to remove one's self from the discriminatory world of blackness. Think Tiger Woods. If he can identify as a social construction combo—well, then, no one should call him a nigger, but they have. No one should joke about him being lynched, but they have. Woods rejected being labeled the first black golfer to win the Masters and actively divorced himself from the black community—even when he benefited from being one of few black Americans in golf. And let's go back to the amazingly talented Mariah Carey, who, at the beginning of her career, ranted she was mixed, with just a pinch of black. When record sales spiraled downward and she began to lose her pop audience, Mimi wondrously found her blackness. Some reports claim Carey's ambiguous racial identity in her early career was at the insistence of her record label.

Is claiming mixed or biracial identity a sociological attempt at gaining privilege? Maybe the true reason Taye Diggs doesn't want his son to be labeled is because he doesn't want his child to be treated with the bias associated with blackness. Tiger Woods fights his blackness because he doesn't want to be called "nigger." Mariah's racial journey was complicated because marketing herself as the "mixed" girl was more profitable than marketing herself as the "black" girl. Brown people are stretching themselves across like a bridge for a piece of that white privilege, even if it's just a few shades browner.

This fight for privilege channels black Americans' complex relationship with color. We've all heard this one: "If this were slavery, all the light-skinned folks would be in the house and the dark-skinned folks would be in the fields!" The light-skinned house slave is a myth. The selection of house and field slaves was rarely based on skin tone; it was based on the relationship with the master. If you were a good, obedient slave, you could make it to the house. Furthermore, most of the lighter-skinned slaves were the bastard children of the master. The mistress of the house wanted those children as deep in the fields as possible. No one received a pass from the horrors of chattel slavery simply because they were lighter-skinned. This is another invented piece of incorrect history that fuels many of the light-skinned versus dark-skinned issues in the black community.

Today, everyone wants to be a tragic mulatto, not knowing the history. The mulatto is a classic stereotype that first made an appearance in nineteenth-century American literature. Eventually this archetype became box-office gold for films like 1934's *Imitation of Life* and 1949's *Pinky*. Troubled characters who stumbled through life in a racially tortured turmoil. Were they black? Were they white? No one accepted them. They were eternal victims, all because mommy and daddy didn't stick to their own kind. Although these characters lived tragic lives, at the same time they were praised as an "exotic" mix and somehow revered as being better than plain ole black.

"Mulatto" is a slave word meaning the result of the mating of a donkey and a horse, otherwise known as a mule—and mules are sterile. Race psychology, which was developed by pseudoscientists to perpetuate intraracial divisions within the black community, still functions today. "Mixed" and "biracial" are simply remixed versions of terms like "mulatto," "quadroon," and "octoroon."

In America, your experiences as male, female, black, white, gay, poor, or middle-class shape who you are. For me, I have never identified as biracial, which is a term that wasn't widely used when I was born in the late 1970s. Even today, "biracial" is not a legal racial identity; it's a pop-culture identity. The concept of biracial identity became mainstream in the late 1980s and early 1990s. In many ways, "biracial" is viewed as a step up from blackness, a cue from Creoles who once upon a time believed they shouldn't adhere to Jim Crow laws because they allegedly weren't black. Jim Crow clapped back with, "Hell no!"

As actress Paula Patton, the daughter of an interracial union, said, "I find [the term] *biracial* offensive. It's a way for people to separate themselves from African Americans, a way of saying, 'I'm better than that.'" Again, fighting for privilege, which is dangerous and exclusionary. My experience is of being black in America, as someone who has endured incalculable amounts of racism. I was never perceived as half and half. Moreover, once I understood race, there was no tragic "confusion" or racial identity issues. I knew I was black, because I had no choice, like most black Americans.

The rant that Nahla, Halle's daughter, or Walker, Taye's son, is not "full black" proves how sadly far behind we are in understanding race. No black Americans are "full black." (No white Americans are "full white," for that matter.) There's no such thing as being "full" any race. Lesson number one in black studies: Being "mixed" is consistent with the black American experience.

Many want to turn me and others of my background into the classic tragic mulatto. My racial identity is not tragic. This isn't a scene from *Imitation of Life*. My theme song isn't Mahalia Jackson's "Trouble of the World," with me running to a casket screaming, "Mama!" This isn't an excerpt from *Queen,* and I will not be hollering, "I'se nig'ra! I'se nig'ra!" Race is not an individual choice; it's a social choice. The key question for anyone with a black and white parent is, "Do you or do you not have white privilege?" If you don't, then you are a black person in America. (Race clearly changes and functions differently outside of the United States, especially in a Latin or Brazilian context.) If Halle Berry's daughter were white or could truly exist in this country under the label of "biracial," then there would be no volatile discussion about her color. As Halle told *Ebony*, "I had to decide for myself, and that's what she's going to have to decide—how she identifies herself in the world. And I think, largely, that will be based on how the world identifies her. That's how I identified myself."

I understand the need for people who have different-race parents to live under racial duality; in many ways we all do. Again, no one is pure black or white, but terms like "mulatto," "quadroon," and "octoroon" failed for a reason. America does not need another divisive racial category, like "biracial," for people to push themselves into.

For me, I am rooted in all of my identities. You might be surprised that I don't cry the narrative of, "The white kids didn't accept me! The black kids didn't accept me!" I am aware this is the discourse of some so-called biracial people, which I can empathize with. However, my melanin is as natural and layered as my gender and sexuality. My passage through racial identity lands me here, in complete harmony with the nuances of blackness.

2 1

COLORED GIRL
TRYING TO STAY
IN THE HOUSE

YOU LEARN DISTINCT SURVIVAL SKILLS WHEN YOU ARE the only "one" in the room, be that the boardroom, classroom, or courtroom. My grandfather taught me this lesson early on. Born in 1923, my granddaddy grew up in Virginia, in the Jim Crow South. As a black man, he witnessed horrific racism: police brutality, lynchings, and rural poverty. "There are a lot of dead colored men in the lakes of Virginia that no one will ever know about," he would say to me. Disgusted by the South's racism, my grandfather joined the Navy and only returned to Virginia for visits. In 1946, Granddaddy landed in Philadelphia to begin a new life.

My grandfather had six kids and two marriages; both of his wives died of complications from obesity. That said, Granddaddy, who never finished high school, was seriously proud of his thirty-year job at SEPTA, Philadelphia's public transportation system. For a black man to be gainfully employed from the 1950s to the 1980s with a job that included benefits, sick days, and retirement—my granddaddy hit the economic lottery. He felt safe through every decade of political turmoil in Philadelphia, owned his house, provided for his family, and taught me the importance of being proudly frugal. "Cheap people always have money! Remember that!"

In the late 1980s, I attended my grandfather's retirement party, which was full of old Italian men who spoke highly of him. "We're going to miss you. Best worker we ever had," many of them complimented him. This was the first time I saw my grandfather around a group of white men. Granddaddy was not meek—quite the contrary, he was bold, loud—but in this moment, he was uncharacteristically passive. "Thank you, sir," he answered simply, nodding his head. "I'll miss y'all, too."

He was lying. There was a basic mistrust my grandfather felt for any white person, and rightfully so. He clearly suffered from post-traumatic stress syndrome after growing up in the Jim Crow South. As we drove away after Granddaddy's retirement party, he reflected, "Yeah, they were some good white folks."

No more than ten years old, I laughed and asked, "What do you mean, Granddaddy?"

"I've met all types of white folks in my life. Never thought I'd meet a good one for a long time, but when you meet some good white folks, you stick with it. Now, look at me. I'm retiring. I'm a colored boy who came from nothing. I own my house, took care of my kids. I did good. My mama would be proud. Glad I found those good white folk." Even as a child, I was disturbed how Granddaddy attributed his success to "good white folk." What about the work he accomplished? The endless overtime? The racial digs? Granddaddy successfully retired because he put in the work, not because of "good white folks." Granddaddy chuckled, "I ain't been a field hand in years."

"A field hand?" I repeated.

"Yeah, the bottom of the barrel. Doing all the rough work and getting nothing in return. Every colored man wants to be in the house…or own the house." My grandfather sighed. "White folks gonna always have power. Not all white folks are bad, it ain't their fault. It's the way their daddy and their daddy's daddy did before them. Colored folks gonna always be left behind. When you start working, you'll see! But Lord knows they were some good white folk at SEPTA." I didn't quite understand what Granddaddy meant at the time, but I would soon learn. Plantation life was always about economics, and, in many ways, the hierarchy of the field hand, house Negro, and free man exists today. Nobody wants to be a field hand.

My grandfather died in 1999, when I was already living in the New York City area, trying to make my way. By 2001, I was twenty-four, Clinton's legacy of mass incarceration permanently demolished cities, the Bush era was beginning to ruin America's economy, and there was no end in sight for Don't Ask, Don't Tell and DOMA (the Defense of Marriage Act). I was still closeted to many people in my life, but when I landed my first real job in Manhattan at a nonprofit organization that catered to diverse communities, I finally felt freedom in the workplace. Many of the employees were openly lesbian, gay, bisexual, and transgender. It was incredible to work at a place where I didn't stress about my sexual orientation. However, the nonprofit organization was 90 percent white and male. Most of the other brown people worked on the janitorial staff; I was an administrative assistant. There was one other black gay man, William, who was in his late forties and held a senior director position. We bonded instantly.

William was completely immersed in the white gay community. His boy-friend of many years was white; he lived in Chelsea, which was the white gayborhood at the time; and although he was from Mississippi, he talked and walked the language of privileged white gay men. Sometimes I judged William as a self-hating black gay man, worshipping the trophy of white gayness, but he always surprised me. His white coworkers and boyfriend never knew that William would casually stroll by my desk and say with a scratchy whisper, "I hate white people!" This one-liner equally shocked and amused me.

William lived in multiple worlds as well and, being more than twenty years older than me, was fully aware he was a black gay man from Mississippi who made something of himself in the Big Apple. He was comfortable in the access he'd achieved, but he didn't have a case of amnesia.

His white coworkers, even those who held lower positions than him, often treated William like "the help." He was randomly called on to make a run to the store, take notes for a meeting, prepare epic presentations in minutes, and serve as a liaison between other departments because "William can talk to people better!" Yes, the brown mouthpiece, which wasn't a true representation of the organization, but presented an illusion of inclusiveness. The organization, like many nonprofits, was constantly criticized for not being diverse. William was the token, and he was well aware.

William came to me one day, quickly closed the office door to ensure no one was in earshot, pulled up a chair next to my desk, and exclaimed, "I need a vacation from white people!"

I laughed and pointed out, "But William, your boyfriend is white."

"Child, I know, but he doesn't get it. I love him. Lord knows I do, but talking to him about his people is like talking to niggas about fried chicken, they just can't separate the two!"

"You're a mess…"

"But I have an issue. I have to go on this damn senior directors' retreat, and I just can't do it this year. I can't. I can't do a full weekend with them."

"Isn't that mandatory?"

"It is, and I got to find a way out of it." The retreat was held the upcoming weekend. I couldn't see a way for William to avoid attending. All the senior directors were required to show their faces and discuss new programs, budgets, and branding. William promised he would find a way out of the retreat. The following Monday, he pulled me into the bathroom, checked that the stalls were empty, and said, "I didn't go!"

"How did you get out of it?" I asked.

"I had that twenty-four-hour flu—very Joan Crawford at the Oscars! They were mad as hell but I didn't hear anything about it today. I know I'll never be able to get away with that again, but thank God I didn't have to go this year!"

"William, I don't get it. Why do you stay here if you dislike these white people so much?"

William stared at me like my eyeballs popped out of my skull. He explained in the deepest Southern drawl I ever heard come out of his mouth, "I got it good! I come and go as I please, they listen to me, I take vacation when I want—ain't nothing about this I want to change. I've had other jobs and I was a field hand. Right now," he said, laying his hand on my shoulder, "I'm just a colored girl trying to stay in the house!"

"A colored girl trying to stay in the house!" I repeated, my laughter echoing in the bathroom.

"That's right!"

"I never heard anyone put it quite that way. My grandfather would say something similar and I always thought he wasn't giving himself enough credit. But now I get it; you know the system...just a colored girl trying to stay in the house," I repeated again.

"Exactly! You gonna learn!" William's mindset wasn't politically correct, and for some, it might appear generational. Yet this is the reality of being black in the workplace. You are trying to stay in the house until you can buy your own freedom.

I left the nonprofit a few years later and in many ways managed to get a free Negro pass by freelancing all over New York City, refusing to take staff positions, regardless of money, and building my own brand. William left the nonprofit as well and eventually retired, living a luxurious life. That colored girl now has her own house.

GOD

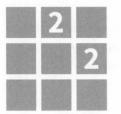

HOLLER IF
YOU HEAR ME

IN NOVEMBER OF 2014, I APPEARED ON HUFFPOST LIVE to discuss a young man who was allegedly "delivered" from homosexuality. I slammed the black church for its hypocrisy by explaining, "If you want to find a whole bunch of black gay folks, just go to the black church. The black church wouldn't even exist without gay people." My rant went viral; I received tons of support from individuals who suffered from spiritual and theological violence in their churches. I pitched *Holler If You Hear Me: Black and Gay in the Church* to BET.com, and I was soon in Atlanta, Georgia, filming a documentary that I created, produced, and directed. I fundamentally knew there was a story. A story I lived and experienced.

"God, I hope this goes well," I whispered to myself as my crew and I drove to the Lost-n-Found Youth homeless shelter in Atlanta. It was May 20, 2015, and Lost-n-Found was the first stop on our vigorous shooting schedule. My nerves rattled as I felt my own past rising in my soul. I was immediately reminded of days living in shelters, enduring abuse from the pulpit, and wrestling with my identities—I wasn't far removed from the young people I was about to meet.

Once we pulled into the driveway of Lost-n-Found, I noticed a young woman on the porch with a cane in one hand, a profound scar etched on the side of her face, and a cigarette between her fingers. I opened the car door and locked eyes with her. "Are you Hannah?" I asked.

"Yeah, that's me," she answered, taking a puff from her Newport.

"I'm so happy to see you," I said. She looked at me, seemingly confused that anyone would be happy to see her. I understood her confusion. She wasn't sure if I could be trusted. When you are marginalized and disenfranchised, anyone could be a predator. Yet, Hannah and I connected.

A month before, I'd had an in-depth conversation with the residential manager of Lost-n-Found, and he thought Hannah would be perfect for the documentary. Her story was heartbreaking: She struggled with her identities, was homeless, and sadly, her best friend, who was transgender, shot himself at eighteen years old. Her story was a study in how the residuals of spiritual and theological violence can affect a life. After the cameras stopped rolling, I thanked her for the interview, and she said, reflecting on the epic story she'd revealed, "I didn't think I would live through this."

Her words collided in my heart. From being a child in an oppressive and racist Washington State, to moving to West Philadelphia to live with my father, knowing I was an embarrassment because he hated that I was gay—and let me know it every day. I wasn't man enough, I wasn't a "black man" enough. I reached out to the church only to be wounded by haunting dogmas. I felt invisible. If you are not being seen or heard, you are not being loved.

My first experiences with faith were as a child in Washington State. Far from religious, my mother insisted I would not be raised with repressive doctrines. Sadly, her own family had been destroyed when her mother became a devout Jehovah's Witness. Family members weren't allowed to speak to each other, and some became "disassociated" for random infractions—even her mother was disassociated for smoking cigarettes. Her family never reconciled after the attack of the Witnesses. When a Jehovah's Witness randomly knocked on our door, my always-colorful mother would yell, "Get away from my house! Y'all fucked up my life enough!"

One summer, my mother agreed to let me attend a Christian camp for a week. My childhood friend, who was also my neighbor, was attending, and I so badly wanted to go with him. However, the fee was outrageous, and my mother was concerned about a religious camp. My friend's parents assured my mother that the camp was run by Christians, not fanatical Bible beaters, and they offered to pay my fee. My mom eventually gave in after I begged for weeks.

With excitement, I traveled with a group of twenty kids deep into the woods of Washington State—the only brown boy of the bunch. With a huge staff of young people in their late teens and early twenties, the camp was glamorous to my welfare-accustomed eyes: nonstop food, a mini recreational room, a massive church, and epic portraits of a blonde-haired, blue-eyed Christ at every turn. Although we enjoyed a few days of games and camp- fires, I soon realized that the camp focused less on summer games and more on the vengeance of God, sinful music (especially the Madonna and Prince I loved), the demonic forces in video games like Super Mario Brothers, and anything under the blood-filled sun of Revelations. By night one, those upper-class Christian whites scared the good-golly-Jim-Crow-Jesus out of me. Death, destruction, fire, and brimstone loomed ahead.

On our last night, we sat on metal folding chairs in a dark, carpeted base- ment with no windows and a musty smell that reeked of a dungeon. We were encouraged to confess our childhood sins. The staff stood stoically before us children, reading the most horrific scriptures in a monotone yet terrifying voice. Fearing we would burn in hell, the children cried about Jesus and promised never to sin again. Kids hollered and trembled with the supposed love of Christ.

When I returned home, I cried to my mom for days about the fear of hell. I even considered throwing out all of my beloved Prince and Madonna albums to guarantee my salvation, threatening to only listen to Amy Grant. "Amy fuckin' Grant?" I remember my mother yelling to one of her friends on the phone. "That is a *true* sin!" My mother was enraged; she knew how religion ruined her family, and she had gone against her better judgment by allowing me to attend the camp.

My mother phoned our "Christian" neighbors and gave them a Jersey- style curse-out so severe, according to my best friend, it left his mother in tears. I thought she was crying because my mother was too mean, but my best friend explained, "No, she told me she's never heard such language come out of a woman's mouth. She knew your mother was going to hell and that broke her heart." I quickly told my mom and was banned from speaking to my best friend again. His family decided my mother and I were tawdry sinners while they were simply spreading the love of Christ. That was my last experience with religion in the white community. Upper-class white religious families come with the resources to send their kids to expensive camps to indoctrinate them. In the black community, the tools to brainwash children, though not as extravagant, are far more creative.

By my early teens I lived in West Philadelphia, strikingly different from Washington State. Before I moved to the City of Brotherly Love, I visited often. I was always shocked by the number of churches in the neighborhoods.

Almost every corner hosted a church along with drug dealers, prostitutes, and alcoholics. I questioned why they would spend so much time around a church. Weren't they embarrassed? I soon learned these "degenerates" marked their territory on church corners because that was where they could make the most cash. The hookers garnered plenty of clients who attended and worked at the church. The drug dealers sold their crack, weed, and other substances to members of the congregation. And alcohol, well, of course everyone was getting their drink on. This "place of worship" fit right in with the street urchins. Pastors would damn prostitutes to hell every Sunday, but lie down with them later that night.

My cousin, Althea, became deeply involved in one of the underground churches in Philly, which were all the rage during the early nineties. Some-one decided that God spoke to them, and *abracadabra*, they were ready to save souls. So I followed Althea, who insisted I attend one of the "services." I had been to black churches before, but never something as underground as the "event" I witnessed in a row house—a far cry from the ritzy Christian camp in Washington State. Once again, I found myself in a dark room listening to a zombie roaring about the love of Christ. The many girls—and few boys, who clearly fit anyone's stereotypical perception of gayness—were packed into a living room with furniture pushed against the walls, dim lighting, and a large picture of white Jesus sitting on a table. A black woman shrieked the Word, gripping her tattered Bible, shaking it at the ceiling, and asking if we wanted to burst into flames. Unlike the monotone voices of the whites at the Christian camp, this "preacher" was filled with rage. "Satan is everywhere! Everywhere!" she hollered, her eyeballs manically bouncing in their sockets. "He's gonna get ya if ya don't repent fo' yo' sins! Repent, children, or burn in the furnace of hell!"

Her wild rants continued until, one by one, everybody got "da spirit." Teens jumped, screamed, spoke in tongues, and dropped to the dirty red-vel-vet-carpeted floor. I scanned the room but remained quiet, praying intensely that I wouldn't be forced to throw myself onto the filthy carpet. Suddenly, Althea caught the spirit, too, and flung her arms in the air, shrieked from her throat, and writhed on the floor. However, she moved her head back and forth ever so softly, and I knew why—she'd just gotten her hair done, and no amount of spirit would ruin her fresh magenta finger waves!

I stood still, along with another girl, but I didn't want to be the only one standing. I felt like I was in middle school, picked last for the kickball team.

I didn't want people to think Christ picked me last! So I decided it was time for me to perform. Faking the Holy Ghost, I threw my arms up, babbled in tongues, fell to the floor (scuffing my new white Reeboks), and shook it up like a Patti LaBelle drag queen. Althea hollered and grabbed onto me because I'd finally gotten the spirit. She held me to her bosom as if we were Jesus and Mary. Everybody was so proud that she'd brought me; I was special. We were then ordered to pay ten dollars.

In the intro to *Holler If You Hear Me: Black and Gay in the Church,* I say: "The church is the root of African American culture." The black church provided safe spaces for black Americans to gather without the presence of whites. That said, today, I believe that many—not all—sectors of the black church are losing relevance and compassion and are steeped in oppression.

I am not an atheist, but I am no Christian either. As Dr. Hubert Harrison, a member of the Socialist Party during the Harlem Renaissance, once stated, "Any black person who accepts orthodox Christianity needs to have his head examined. I refuse to worship a lily-white God and a Jim Crow Jesus." Following Dr. Harrison's line of reasoning, some of these church members need CAT scans.

In the summer of 2005, I landed my first professional writing assignment. I wrote an article titled "Black, Gay, and Beyond HIV," and trekked to the soul of Brooklyn for a story on an organization called People of Color in Crisis (POCC), which is now closed.

POCC was one of few organizations in New York City reaching out to gay and bisexual men of color who were infected with HIV/AIDS. Formed in 1988 by black American and West Indian gay men who were concerned about the lack of HIV/AIDS awareness in the black community, POCC provided numerous services, including group meetings, testing, and counseling.

I spoke to Michael Roberson, the director of services, a passionate man who had been fighting for LGBT rights even back when I was a teenager in Philadelphia. I will never forget what he said during our interview: "We live in a black community that's systematically homophobic. Black gay people live in communities where they operate out of a place of invisibility, which is detrimental to their own growth." He added, "For communities of color that are very God-centered, the most detrimental thing you can tell somebody is that the Supreme Being views you as an abomination. Where can you go from there? If that is the case, then why ask someone to wear a condom to protect a life that they have been told is of no value?" It was a sentiment I'd always felt, but had never put into words.

In November of 2006, an acquaintance in my neighborhood suddenly died. He was just a few months away from his thirtieth birthday. A black gay man, he was well known in the club scene; he had a beautiful smile and always greeted me with warm energy. His death was a complete shock. We were the same age, and while we were not close friends, he lived in my neighborhood and I would see him weekly.

I attended his funeral with my best friend, Nikki. I had some concerns, because it was rumored that people in his immediate family were angry with all the "gay people" calling their home. I never knew how true that was, but I assumed a grieving family would put their differences aside for the untimely passing of a twenty-nine-year-old man. Before I went to the service, I told myself I would leave my political beliefs at the beat-up church door. I hadn't been to a church in years, and I was showing my respect for a friend, not joining the choir.

The bishop—a title he didn't deserve—began his eulogy while perched in a massive, glitzy chair with rhinestones, fake gold, and an ostentatious sparkle. His hypocritical throne posed a stark contrast to the tiny church in shambles. Once the bishop hit the slippery soapbox, he ranted everything short of "All faggots are going to hell!" He belted out scripture and declared, "If you don't have the key to Jesus, you're going to hell! I know there are brothers and sisters in here who don't agree, but you will be judged! It ain't too late to save yourself!" He pointed to my friend's shell of a body in the coffin. "He don't have another chance." He yelled the classic, trite line, "If you accept Jesus, you will be washed white as snow!" *White as snow? What conversion therapy is this?* I thought.

There was no hint of compassion or sincerity in the bishop's toxic voice. This man of the church barely mentioned my friend's name. This wasn't a eulogy; it was a condemnation, a narcissistic sermon to preach his oppressive beliefs. More disturbing were the deacons, seated right behind me, cosigning with a "Well!" "Amen!" "Hallelujah!" I could tell some of them were gay. *I know a self-hating, brainwashed church homo when I see one*, I thought.

Nikki and I sat angrily stewing in the pews. A tear fell from my left eye, not for our friend who had passed, but because of the astronomical level of hatred I heard at the service. A eulogy is to celebrate the life and accomplishments of the deceased, not to damn them to hell. I've attended funerals for convicted criminals where no one spewed the language I heard that day. As we sat there for a sermon that was more than twenty minutes long, I whispered to Nikki, "I couldn't imagine hearing this as a child or teen, knowing I was gay." This aggressive display of hate from the deacons, nodding their heads in unison to the pontificating preacher, could damage someone for life. I'd certainly grappled with my sexuality as a child, but the blatant spiritual violence I witnessed at my friend's funeral was not part of my upbringing.

That experience was clear proof that for black folks to move forward, we must challenge the agenda of the black church in terms of sexuality. It is one of the most poisonous aspects of our community. One would be shocked how much the agendas of some black churches have in common with conservative, racist groups—on issues of sexuality, gender identity, and interracial relationships. Some black churches have uncomfortable bedfellows rooted in oppression. Don't be appalled if your homophobic church marches at an anti–gay marriage rally and a good old boy from Alabama is walking right next to the reverend and his wife. Yes, anti-gay beliefs are funded by whites, but there is a common dominator that links racist whites and homophobic blacks—religion. These were not the ideas of African religions, but are a direct result of Eurocentric Christianity.

This is not an assault on conservative Christians. Instead, this is a call for a panoramic view into the structural underpinnings of the use of religion as a tool of oppression. The faithful Christians and the gays who cosign are equally a part of this oppressive fabric. Sure, not everyone who is anti-gay or opposes equal rights for LGBT people is hateful, but the lobotomized who follow the super-cult of religion have no idea they are being fed microwaved soul food. Being religious does not make you a zombie, but following the dogma of church queens like Bishop Eddie Long, alleged ex-gays like Donnie McClurkin, or your everyday preacher, who is neither a historian or therapist, can land you a never-ending role in *Night of the Living Dead*. Spiritual development unfolds and regenerates itself in various ways through different periods of human existence and cultures. The current construct of religion is a spiritual mini-mall. Nothing handcrafted, just an assembly line of reversible, matching little outfits for the spirit, attaching shame to the human potential for spiritual ascendance and transcendence.

Nearly every black gay man I know who grew up in a religious household still suffers from the aftermath of spiritual violence. For me, being gay saved my life. If I were straight, I would probably be dead, incarcerated, or saddled with out-of-wedlock children, like most of the boys I grew up with in West Philadelphia. Being gay made me introverted as a child, forcing me to stay home and study rather than hang out on street corners. I prepared myself for a life that I knew was bigger than constantly being bullied or called a faggot by classmates or some family members. I wouldn't be the writer I am if I were straight. I would not appreciate art, music, and literature in the way I do if I were heterosexual. Being gay is an identity that helped me flourish.

One day in 1998, during my first year in the New York City area, I was walking through Harlem and saw a shirt in a window that stopped me on the street. The black shirt with white letters read, "A real black man is a man who loves God. A real black man is a man who doesn't deal drugs. A real black man is a man who doesn't have sex with men." I was only twenty-one but already secure in my sexual identity. The words didn't hit me in the same way they must have assaulted many others that day. Disappointingly, engaging in homophobia in the black community equaled becoming a "real man." I rejected that notion. I am black. I am a man. My sexual orientation is not my damnation, but my saving grace.

At the end of *Holler If You Hear Me: Black and Gay in the Church*, I quote James Baldwin: "Because I was raised in a Christian culture, I never considered myself to be a totally free human being." You can only survive in bondage for so long. We aren't all as resilient as Mr. Baldwin. The intent of my work is to free someone.

CHURCH QUEEN

ON A LATE NIGHT IN OCTOBER 2007, I STEPPED OFF THE A train in Harlem, ready to interview "Rob," Donnie McClurkin's ex-lover. I was surprised Rob agreed to speak with me. Sure, McClurkin's recent rampages against gays were getting more over-the-top than ever, but "spilling the tea" on a pastor was against the code of church queen culture.

Existing in vacuums of hypocrisy, church queen culture is a vital part of the black church and the black community. Most church queens are clearly not heterosexual by anyone's view, but members in churches turn a blind eye. Church queens live, breathe, and die the "don't ask, don't tell" policy in their houses of worship.

Church queens are in the choir, in the pulpit, and baking the sweet potato pie, and they pride themselves on being "good" Christians. They believe they are going to burn in a fiery depths of a Christian hell, yet they get their guts banged out on a regular basis and partake in the most decadent sexual happenings that would make even the biggest whores say, "Well, damn— maybe I need to go to church if I can get this much sex there!"

Church queens argue that being gay is only "temporary" and one day they will wake up with an unforgettable vagina on their mind. This mindset is understandable; it is the aftershocks of years of theological violence. It's hard being in your early twenties and going through "gay puberty" (trying to get over the hate you feel for yourself), but when you're knocking on thirty's door and have been dating men for years, it's pathetic. Sure, some might manage to engage in sex with a few women—which somehow allows these men to desperately clutch onto the last remains of their heterosexuality.

These men are oftentimes misogynistic, minimizing women as babymaking machines. They make statements like, "If this gay thing doesn't work out, then I'll just get with a woman, get married, and have some kids." As if church queens are going to step out of a gay club and find some random woman waiting for them with legs open, saying: "Dive right in!"

Just being gay and in the church doesn't automatically make you a self-hating church queen. I have plenty of friends who are openly gay in their churches, attend services with their boyfriend or husband, and are loved and appreciated. They participate in institutions that honor them, with leaders who don't use the trite line of, "We don't judge! You're just like the prostitute or the murderer!" There's nothing to judge, because their lives are not sinful.

On the other hand, I know people who are openly gay and still support churches that are damning gays to hell. Their excuse is, "Well, I'm not like the church queens—I'm open!" Yes, but you are complicit in the viciousness of homophobia in the black church.

That said, I'd thought Rob was a card-carrying church queen. I had known him for years. He gave me vocal lessons when I was attempting to pursue a career in music. Rob was a staple in the gospel music industry, having sung backup for many artists. His voice was massive, his musical ear near perfect.

Early in our friendship he was in an unstable relationship and refused to say the person's name. The person wasn't calling, was rejecting him, and he hated it. Rob was not a young man; he was tired of dating games. In one of our long conversations I mocked him for not telling me the person's name. "Why are you so secretive?" I quizzed.

Trusting me, Rob admitted the guy was in the gospel music industry. I wasn't a huge fan of current gospel, but there was one artist I knew of, and coincidentally I had just seen a video for the song "We Fall Down." I remembered watching the video and saying to myself, "Who the hell is this church queen?" I asked Rob if I could take a guess. He said sure, but stressed that I wouldn't know because I wasn't familiar with gospel music. Confidently, I guessed, "Is it Donnie McClurkin?"

Rob paused. "How did you guess?"

"I just saw his music video and he looked like a big old queen to me!" We both laughed.

Rob felt comfortable. I was probably the only person outside of his gospel circle who knew of his relationship with Donnie McClurkin—years before

I became a professional writer. Rob would call me when he was rejected by Donnie, had been stood up, or was waiting for his call. I encouraged him to leave the man alone. Then I began to hear about McClurkin's homophobic rants. McClurkin claimed he was an ex-gay and was only gay because he was molested. This was shocking to me since I knew his on-and-off boyfriend.

I grew tired of hearing about the trials of Rob and Donnie. Eventually, I pulled back from Rob. Plus, I could tell he was uncomfortable with some of my views on religion. As in many cases of religious people grappling with identity, if I ever challenged Rob on his beliefs, he couldn't answer me. Any conversation questioning why he was wrapped up in an institution consistently damning him to hell was chalked up to, "You don't have faith."

In 2004, I attempted to date someone who was not a gospel singer but heavily involved in the church. It was short-lived, but in a heated argument over religion, Donnie McClurkin came up. This person insisted Donnie McClurkin was an ex-gay. I laughed and said I knew Donnie McClurkin's boyfriend. He pressed me for a name, I gave a few details and eventually said "My friend Rob." I didn't think he knew Rob; he seemed to believe me and eventually changed the subject.

Days later, Rob called me, enraged that I'd told someone about him and Donnie. I didn't know the guy I was seeing knew Rob, but I'd forgotten how church queens stuck together. Rob said that he trusted me and told me how wrong it was for me to bring up his personal life just to make a point about religion. I apologized—although, I stressed, if they were not immersed in this creepy "church queen" code, then the conversation wouldn't have happened. If Donnie McClurkin and others weren't trying to be the poster children for how to remain hetero, especially when it was a lie, then there wouldn't be secrecy and shame. My friendship with Rob, of course, tapered off even more.

In 2007, future president Barack Obama was supportive of the LGBT community, but at the time was against same-sex marriage. During the Logo channel's LGBT debate in August 2007, Obama said, "I'm somebody who I think is willing to talk about these issues even when it's hard—in front of black ministers." Many wondered if Obama could find a manageable middle ground between two divided groups—the black church and the LGBT community. At that point, the answer was yes.

Things began to unravel in early October 2007 when Obama's "Embrace the Change" gospel concert series announced Hezekiah Walker, Byron

Cage, and other gospel greats as part of the lineup. There was also the contemporary sister duo Mary Mary, who, in my interview with them in March 2007, encouraged gays and lesbians to "align themselves with the Bible" and compared the LGBT community to murderers. The most problematic addition, however, was Donnie McClurkin, a self-proclaimed ex-gay who "counseled" youth about converting from homosexuality.

Donnie McClurkin was arguably the most famous and profitable face in gospel music at the time. The "We Fall Down" hitmaker was a two-time Grammy winner and pastor of Perfecting Faith Church in Freeport, New York. In addition, McClurkin was a prominent voice in the conservative black community, a demographic Obama had yet to grab.

Some in the LGBT community were perplexed about how Obama could be for equal rights yet employ the likes of Donnie McClurkin. In an effort at damage control, Obama's camp released a statement in late October saying they had been unaware of McClurkin's beliefs and admitted that the ex-gay's comments on homosexuality were "deeply hurtful and offensive to many Americans." However, it went on to say, "At the same time, a great many African Americans share Pastor McClurkin's beliefs. This also cannot be ignored."

McClurkin claimed he "prayed the gay away," and at the final installment of the gospel concert series in October 2007, he offered, "I tell you that God delivered me from homosexuality." For the LGBT community, the "Embrace the Change" lineup seemed contradictory from Obama, who referred to the LGBT community as his "gay brothers and sisters." Furthermore, the lineup wasn't much of a change from the president at the time, George W. Bush. Mary Mary and Donnie McClurkin performed for President George Bush in 2005. President Bush was staunchly anti–gay marriage, even advocating for a constitutional amendment to ban marriage equality. Political strategists argue that Bush won the 2004 election on his "biblical" beliefs.

In 2004, on the Christian Broadcasting Network—Pat Robertson's organization—McClurkin said, "I'm not in the mood to play with those who are trying to kill our children." In Donnie McClurkin's 2001 book *Eternal Victim, Eternal Victor*, he wrote: "The abnormal use of my sexuality continued until I came to realize that I was broken and that homosexuality was not God's intention...for my masculinity." *For my masculinity?* According to McClurkin, God himself now had a hand in so-called gender norms? The line sounded like serious self-hate. Then, on October 22, 2007, McClurkin told the Associated Press, "I don't believe that [homosexuality] is the intention of God. Sexuality, everything is a matter of choice."

Tired of the hypocrisy, I reconnected with Rob. I asked if he was still in a relationship with Donnie. He revealed that he ended his relationship with Donnie three years earlier, in 2004. He heard Donnie's recent rants and was disappointed. I delicately asked if he would be interested in doing an anonymous interview about his relationship with Donnie McClurkin.

I have never endorsed outing people, but in situations where you are spewing homophobia, yet having sex with men, I felt it was fair. I thought Rob would instantly say no, but he said he would think about it and call me back. The next day he called and agreed to do the interview, as long as it was anonymous. He explained that McClurkin was a very powerful person in the gospel industry, and Rob wouldn't want his career ruined. I asked, "Don't you think he'll be able to tell it is you once he reads the interview?"

"No," he replied. "Because there are so many other men he has been with. I am one of a million." Late on a Thursday night, I made my way to Rob's apartment in Harlem, and he revealed every detail of his relationship with Donnie. I posted the interview on my blog on October 25, 2007. The story went viral, and very few people doubted its truth. People in the comments of the entry revealed they engaged in recent relationships with Donnie as well.

Did I have actual proof of this relationship? No, but this was not someone I met off the street who said, "Yeah, child, I had a relationship with Donnie McClurkin!" This is someone I had known for years; I was privy to the details of their courtship. I have no sympathy for hypocrites who actively seek to damage others. As Rob revealed the details of their relationship, many of which I heard before, I knew he was telling the truth. Furthermore, I felt in my soul that even if it was revealed to just one person that McClurkin was a fraud, especially if it was a young gay man or woman who was struggling with their sexuality, then I had done something right.

Then there was Bishop Eddie Long, the greatest church queen who ever lived. The Atlanta pastor was known for his vibrant sermons, A-list status among black preachers, and infamous anti-LGBT rants. Long used hate as a platform by preaching of a "homosexual cure" and recruited LGBT people for "sexual reorientation." In 2004, Eddie Long and Bernice King (Dr. King's daughter) went as far as to lead an anti-LGBT march to Dr. Martin Luther King, Jr.'s gravesite. Coretta Scott King, Dr. King's widow, famously spoke out against their bigotry and said her husband would've been pro-LGBT rights.

In 2010, the tables turned on Mr. Long. He was outed by a group of men who claimed he coerced them into engaging in a sexual relationship when they were barely legal. Their testimonies went viral and the bishop settled out of court. Long never outwardly addressed the claims, but the graphic accounts from the men were hard to deny. Furthermore, it was a badly kept secret for years in suburban Atlanta, where Long was the senior pastor at New Birth Missionary Baptist Church, that he led a double life—his church politics didn't match his bedroom.

Eddie Long died of an aggressive form of cancer on January 15, 2017. I don't know who he was as a father, friend, or husband. I don't know if he selectively helped members of his church who fit his spiritual confines of heterosexuality. Nonetheless, Eddie Long's legacy is tainted for eternity. He was a predator and a religious sham. The day he passed away, social media was flooded with Eddie Long's history of hypocritical homophobia. How ironic, Bishop Eddie Long will eternally be associated with "gay"—the very thing he allegedly hated. Look at God!

Church queen culture still thrives, but I pray to whatever gods that will listen for leaders in houses of worship to stop co-signing any type of conversion therapy. As Dr. Kenneth Samuel brilliantly said in my documentary *Holler If You Hear Me: Black and Gay in the Church*, "If we are so right that we are damaging people, it undermines all of our rightness." Thankfully, the backlash for a homophobic rant is epic and can ruin careers. Today, this kind of rhetoric is no longer as marketable and, at the end of the biblical day, pastors want to make money. So they've learned the brutal lessons of their hate. McClurkin was outed by me and Long was outed by a handful of young men in Atlanta. To that I say, all eyes are on the church queens. Hypocrites will not get a pass on discrimination by using the name of Jesus. Not today, Satan. Not today.

INTERSECTIONS

DIVAS LIVE: BEYONCÉ, MARY, AND PATTI

IN SEPTEMBER OF 2007, CHAKA KHAN SAID TO ME IN AN interview, "I want to thank all my gay following, all my people, for staying with me and supporting me all these years. You all have been my most solid fan base and that's the truth." In December of 2008, Brandy Norwood gushed to me during an interview with *The Advocate*, "My gay fans are very, very loyal, and I really respect them for that. They stick with you through it all. If you are going through an uptime or a downtime, they're there." Jennifer Holliday explained to *PrideSource* in 2014, "I used to be able to work with the gay clubs without a record and not work anywhere else. I would go on at 3 or 4 in the morning and they allowed me to hold onto my dignity."

Where would female artists be without their LGBT following, especially black female artists? It's an understated intersection of race, pop culture, sexuality, and gender. Many female artists owe their careers to the undying loyalty of the LGBT community, and the artists I quoted above own it. The LGBT community supports these artists when they can't hit the same notes they once could, when the music isn't selling, and when the mainstream writes them off as "old" because they are over thirty. The LGBT community reveres black women in the entertainment industry and never lets anyone forget their talent.

My breaks in journalism began with LGBT media and its support of black female artists. When *The Advocate*, *HX Magazine,* and other LGBT outlets hired me, I had the privilege of interviewing legends and icons, the artists I had admired for years. I researched and aimed to ask fun, relevant, and smart questions—and to properly serve the audience I was writing for. A topic I always wanted to explore was the fascinating relationship between black female artists and the LGBT community. Why are these female artists gay icons? And is their connection to the LGBT community sincere or marketing?

One of the greatest gay icons of our time is Beyoncé. The voice, the stage performance, and the hair—but her appeal is more than superficial. Her music was the soundtrack for many LGBT youths who struggled with identity, even back in her Destiny's Child days. Everyone from Laverne Cox to Janet Mock cites Queen Bey as an influence on their walk for freedom in their identities.

Full disclosure: I was once a Beyoncé hater. I am not sure when the hate began. I enjoyed her singing and loved her performing, and there was no doubt she was talented. Still, in the early 2000s, she was everywhere—in every commercial, singing every hook, and everyone on the planet simultaneously loved her. It was a Beyoncé nation and I wasn't converted. Part of my exhaustion with her was sparked when after the Madonna and Britney Spears kiss at the 2003 MTV Video Music Awards, Bey allegedly stated she would never kiss a woman on stage because of her religion. The backlash was swift, she quickly released a statement explaining she was misquoted (no actual proof came out that she made the statement) and said, "I have never judged anyone based on his or her sexual orientation and have no intention of starting now. I have a lot of gay and lesbian fans and I love them no differently than my straight fans."

My Beyoncé hateration officially changed after interviewing her when she was only twenty-five years old for a story about 2006's *Dreamgirls*. She was kind, attentive, respectful, and warm—different from other superstars I'd interviewed. I also asked her about the alleged comments from 2003, which she squarely denied. Since *Dreamgirls*, Beyoncé's support of the LGBT community rang true throughout the years. In a 2011 interview with *PrideSource*, she explained: "Most of my audience is actually women and my gay fans, and I've seen a lot of the younger boys kind of grow up to my music." She continued, "I have my [gay] stylists and my makeup artist, and all of their stories and the slang words I always put it in my music. We inspire each other. Like I said, we're one."

Describing the LGBT community and herself as one is a fascinating connection, which goes beyond a fan base. Queen Bey clearly outlined her queer sensibility in 2016's *Lemonade*. Although the project was praised as monumental black feminism, for me and others, the intentional LGBT representation could not be ignored. In the song "Formation," she presented a profoundly queer vision of blackness, opening with Messy Mya asking, "What happened at the New Orleans?" Mya was a popular gender nonconforming YouTube personality who was shot and killed in November 2010. Bey resurrected his voice for one of the most popular songs of 2016.

"Formation" also included Big Freedia, New Orleans native and Queen of Bounce, who is openly gay and gender nonconforming. Beyoncé gestured to an alternative and necessary imagery of blackness. For the queer folks who admired her, she didn't use the LGBT community as content makers, she gave them a narrative and space in her work. Bey is the intersection of black female artistry and queer artistry. Her loyalty to the LGBT community is clearly genuine, and her work has consistently been inclusive, proving pop culture can empower the silenced.

In 2009, Mary J. Blige had a small role in Tyler Perry's *I Can Do Bad All by Myself*, her first movie in eight years. I was covering the press junket for the film and was told Mary would participate in a handful of interviews. To my shock, I was approved to interview the Queen of Hip-Hop Soul. Although I've chatted with many celebrities over the years, there are only a handful of stars I admire like Mary J. Blige. She is an artist who effortlessly connected with the LGBT community. When her second album, *My Life,* debuted in 1994, she resonated with me—not to mention every drag queen in Philadelphia who rocked a blonde, bobbed wig and a metallic bubble coat. Mary was my youth; her music triggered significant moments in my life. Songs like "I Never Wanna Live Without You," "Don't Go," "Be Happy," and the title track eased me through my first love and heartbreak. As an eighteen-year-old in West Philly, I never dreamed that I would meet an artist who sang my life on my CD player.

As a publicist ushered me into a Ritz Carlton hotel room, I did my best to maintain my composure. And there was Mary, talking quietly on the phone, dressed all in black with her toned arms exposed and rocking a short, blonde crop cut. I viewed Mary as a powerhouse, but her frame was unexpectedly delicate. She gave me a slight smile and quickly ended her call by saying, "This interview is about to start. We'll be doing all this press again when the album comes out. I'm so blessed." No cameras. No lighting. Mary's gratitude wasn't an act.

The butterflies in my stomach overwhelmed me. I rarely get nervous, but this wasn't a random starlet or pop singer. This was Mary J. She shook my hand, gave me a wider smile, and like hip-hop soul magic, my nerves calmed. Although I never personally met her before, she made my heart believe that I had. Without trying, Mary made me feel like I was just like her. She was disarming. Her celebrity was gone, a talent most celebrities haven't mastered, bringing herself right down to Earth.

Mary was candid and generous in an interview that ranged from film to music to healing from the demons of her past. In the final two minutes, I knew I needed to seize my moment with her outside of the film. When does a person get to thank an artist, one-on-one, for the music they created? "I came out in 1995 and *My Life* helped me so much," I started. "It just changed me."

Mary nodded her head with each word, staring into my eyes, and slowly replied, "Thank you."

"'When you talked about your life—I felt like you totally got my life."

"Yeah, pretty much nobody knows what you're going through. Absolutely."

Mary told *The Advocate* back in 2007, "The majority of my fans are gay. The majority of them are, and I have to really make sure that they know I'm paying attention to the fact that they support me, and I support them." It's not always big hair, elaborate stage performances, or flowing gowns that garner an LGBT following; it's simply soul, which is the heart of MJB. Through this interview, I was able to thank Mary on behalf of every LGBT person who was helped or even saved by her music over the years.

Before there was Mary and Beyoncé, there was Patti LaBelle. She is arguably the greatest gay icon of all time and a prime example of the intersection of the LGBT community and black female artists. Not just because she's insanely talented, but her loyalty anchors back before it was popular or marketable to have an LGBT fan base, which she clearly expressed to me when I interviewed her at Trump Tower in October of 2007 for her Christmas album, appropriately titled *Miss Patti's Christmas*.

When the soul empress floated into the hotel room, her arms were wide as she sang her 1986 hit "On My Own"—it was the best first impression of Patti any human being could ask for. She was dressed in black, her hair in a bob, and face perfectly done.

"I'm sorry I'm late!" she apologized. As Patti made her way toward me, she acknowledged every single person, complimenting people's hair, bags, and shoes and appreciating the view from the hotel. Patti found beauty in every step.

When the icon sat across from me, I asked if she needed anything. She replied, "Just some water. Some lotion, I'm ashy—or some grease!" she laughed.

We found Patti her lotion and water, and I began, "Miss Patti, my name is Clay and I'm going to be doing some of the gay press."

Patti quickly asked, "So are you gay?"

"I am gay," I responded.

"Well, I was getting ready to look at you!" The room of about ten people, including me, bursted into laughter.

Always ready with a comeback, I responded, "Well, I'm not DL!"

Patti threw her hands in the air and screamed with joy, then sang in her flawless falsetto, "Well, *you can wrap it up!*" She added, "I ain't gonna bother you! I ain't gonna bother you!"

I clarified, "You can bother me!"

"I can? Okay! I'll just be looking."

Our conversation hadn't even started and I already knew this would be one of the best interviews of my career. We talked her latest album, refusing to get more plastic surgery (Patti had a nose job in the 1980s, but told me, "To get stuff taken off you've got to get cut. Do I look like a cutter to you?"), her relationship with the late Phyllis Hyman ("I think she had a feeling she was going to have a short life. She lived like it was her last day."), and her reactions to the singers of today ("These women can come out and do anything, sell records and can't do a show!"). We discussed her church roots and LGBT fan base.

"You also have a religious following in the black church," I began. "Do you have any personal conflicts with your strong ties to the church and your strong ties to the gay community?"

Patti huffed, "That should make no difference. If the church has a problem with that, the church needs to go and see Jesus! The church needs to go and have themselves examined if they're going to judge somebody who is gay. If you're going to put them out because of that then you need to research and find out what's wrong with the church. There are some churches that embrace you and they're not going to forgive you. Why would I forgive you for your sexual orientation? That's awful...judgment."

I followed up with, "So, you don't you think being gay is a sin?"

"I know being gay is not a sin!" she nearly shouted. "If I woke up tomorrow being gay do you think I'd think I was a sinner? Heck, no!" Comments like this were extremely forward-thinking ten years ago. These were the days of the damaging narrative of "You're gay and going to hell—but I still love you!" Affirming language from Miss Patti—in her own style, of course— existed long before the progressive voices of Melissa Harris-Perry, Marc Lamont Hill, Joy-Ann Reid, and Michaela Angela Davis rose to prominence on cable news or social media. Although I was comfortable in my identities, it never hurts to be affirmed.

At the end of the interview, she thanked me for the questions, gave me a big hug, pointed down at a plate full of food, and lovingly demanded, "I need you to eat those salmon and mashed potatoes! I paid too much for this food for it to go to waste!" I proudly chowed down on Patti's leftovers.

As she was leaving, Miss Patti asked me to name some other artists who were adored by the LGBT community. I threw out names like Diana Ross, Janet Jackson, and Madonna. She leaned over with a slight whisper and asked, "But who is the biggest?"

I admitted, "Without a doubt, you are!" Patti tossed both hands to the sky, bolted from her chair, and hopped around in a circle, an image I will never forget.

Not every person in the LGBT community loves their so-called divas. But many of the people I know, including myself, found solace in the goddesses who implicitly and explicitly spoke to them. Maybe it's the prejudice and double standards that black women endure in the entertainment industry, to which LGBT people can relate. When a community is so hungry for representation, Bey's "Formation," Mary's vulnerability, or Patti's gut-wrenching soul (plus her advocacy for HIV/AIDS in the 1980s when President Ronald Reagan refused to say the word) can ease the loneliness of being marginalized. I only hope one day there will be superstars like Beyoncé, Mary, and Miss Patti who can be openly LGBT, presenting their narrative not through "divas," but through their own creativity. Until then, I will bow down to the humble divas who use their talent and fame to uplift a community that passionately uplifts them.

BEHIND THE VELVET ROPE

I MARCHED THROUGH THE COMPLEXITIES OF SEXUALITY, treaded through the constructs of race, disconnected from the capitalistic restraints of faith, and found love in all of my identities. I did the so-called work, attempting to discover the elusive "authentic self." I believed I would never be voiceless, repressed, or owned again. A lifetime of internal work would result in total freedom. I was seriously wrong. Ironically, my career, passion, and livelihood transported me back to a familiar space of repression and fear. Yes, I've been blessed to interview people I truly admire, like Janet Jackson, Wes Craven, Anita Hill, Angela Davis, Mary J. Blige, Lee Daniels, Whoopi Goldberg, and countless others. However, it's not all glamour, especially behind the velvet rope, and the rigors of my "dream job" eventually wore on my soul.

My first year as a journalist, I was living the irony of interviewing millionaires, but not earning a dime. I did the work because I needed the exposure as a writer, and, like in any career, I was paying high-priced dues. Eventually, I gained more access to celebrities, which allowed me to earn enough money to live and eat. By 2009, I landed a regular writing gig for an online media outlet and had the opportunity to interview a legendary rapper who was a contestant on a reality competition program. Although her music was on the decline, which happens to nearly every artist, she was on a popular show that could revive her career. After several days of back and forth with her publicist, we finally secured a date and time for a phone interview. We were set!

I waited with excitement by my phone, questions in hand, ten minutes before our scheduled interview time, ready. Nearly two hours and countless apologies from embarrassed publicists later, I was connected to the hip-hop legend. Her thin voice came on the line—no apologies for being late, just an obvious annoyance at having to do an interview. I steeled myself and asked diverse questions about the reality show—for relevance—and, for substance, hip-hop. I dug into her iconic career, asking about legendary moments, specific lyrics, her die-hard fans, and how her hip-hop roots would translate on the reality show. She sounded pleased that I knew her work so thoroughly. As the conversation progressed, I felt her defenses lowering. She was almost starting to *enjoy* herself.

While researching for the interview, I asked people to submit questions via my blog. The main question I received was: "Please ask her why she got all that crazy plastic surgery! Does she want to look white?" At that time, she never addressed her extensive and extreme surgery, but she clearly changed her entire molecular structure.

There is a delicate balance a journalist must toe with celebrity interviews, between the pressure to ask the questions people want answered and the pressure to never disrespect the artist. I remember once being advised by Kim Osorio, the former editor-in-chief of *The Source* magazine, "Never be afraid to ask a question."

I had transitioned from an unpaid cub reporter to a working celebrity journalist on my ability and willingness to navigate murky celebrity terrain. I was going to honor what my readers wanted. It was how to ask the question that proved challenging. In the past, I'd talked about plastic surgery with Patti LaBelle and Vivica Fox, among others, and drew from those experiences—what worked, what clearly didn't. Therefore, in the nicest voice I could summon, I said, "This is a big question that we got and you can decide if you don't want to answer it. There is a perception in the black community that you didn't like the way you looked as a black woman so you got plastic surgery to make yourself look less black. What's your reaction?"

Click.

She hung up on me.

Seconds later, an extremely nice publicist called and tried to sell me a story that the artist had been rushed off the phone because she was walking into rehearsal. The publicist promised the artist wasn't offended by the question and hadn't disconnected the call. It was clear she had hung up, and I said so to the publicist, who frantically explained, "Oh, she would never hang up, especially after you gave her the option to not answer. *Never.*" The defensiveness in her tone told me otherwise. I published the interview, revealing that she'd abruptly hung up on me, which started a flurry online. Some took her side, others took my side. While the interview was good for page views, I was disappointed. However, the foolishness didn't end there.

Three years later, in May of 2012, I was approached by a different publicist to once again interview the rap icon for her tour, which was making a stop at a venue in the Bronx. Obviously there was a bitter taste in my mouth from our first encounter, but even though she was getting more press for beefing with other rappers than for her significant contribution to the artistic landscape, her talent was undeniable, and, more plainly, I was still a fan. Of course I agreed to do the interview.

She was confirmed for one o'clock on a Friday. This time around, the interview would be on camera for a popular online media outlet. Though I was aware of the shoestring budget, this was going to be one of my first on-camera interviews, so I hired a makeup artist with fifty dollars of my own money. At eleven o'clock in the morning, and immediately after the makeup was finished, I received a call from the publicist, apologizing because the interview had been pushed to five p.m.

My heart sank. *Here we go again*, I thought.

"The interview will definitely happen at five p.m.," the publicist assured me. "*I promise.*"

The cameraperson assigned to accompany me explained he couldn't make a last-minute five p.m. shoot because of a previous engagement. I understood; one p.m. to five p.m. was a huge leap, so instead, the media outlet I was working for hired a video freelancer to travel all the way to the Bronx. Thinking of what occurred three years before, I was doubtful the interview would happen. I called the freelancer and warned, "I don't know what to expect with this interview. We could be waiting for hours." The freelancer agreed to do the interview and said he would wait as long as it took.

A little before three p.m., I phoned the publicist to triple-check that five p.m. would still happen.

"Absolutely!" she reassured me.

I made the arduous trip from lower Manhattan to the Bronx and arrived by four-thirty p.m. The two-person camera crew was already there, and the publicist immediately greeted me at the lobby. As she trotted over with a stiff smile on her face, I saw the artist running into the theater wearing fatigue pants with a Hello Kitty top. Her hair was frizzy and she clearly wasn't in makeup. Nevertheless, the publicist insisted the interview would begin in the next fifteen minutes.

"But she isn't in hair and makeup," I noted, stating the obvious. I did a quick mental calculation and estimated it would take at least two hours for her transformation. "No, we're going to do it *now*," the publicist confirmed with confidence.

By five p.m., the publicist returned with apologies. The rapper needed to conduct a sound check, so our interview wouldn't happen until six p.m. "But, immediately after sound check," she assured us with another tight smile, "I *promise!*" Of course, this wasn't my first rodeo; I had come to expect this, so I accepted—not like I had a choice—and asked if we could record her sound check for B-roll. The publicist thought it was a great idea.

I sat in the fifth row of the venue in the Bronx and watched a hip-hop legend conduct a "sound check." She repeatedly spat lyrics with her thin, high voice, which was too weak for the system as she attempted to match the top and bottom levels. She was clearly frustrated.

"My voice is light!" she hollered, "I need it louder! Louder!" Someone from her crew or the theater, I wasn't sure which, tried to console her and, taking on her frustration, demanded to the engineers at the back of the theater, "We have to get this perfect! It's gotta sound like Whitney Houston is gonna be here!"

Sound technicians frantically struggled to correct the levels. Like headless chickens, her crew scattered around the stage as she plopped down on a speaker and whined about shoes. "Where are my high heels?" she asked someone in her entourage, who looked down and shook her head. "You forgot the shoes?" the icon scolded. "*The shoes?!*" I was waiting for Her Royal Highness to order a beheading.

There was an entourage of people coming in and out like a revolving door. When her dancers joined, they appeared befuddled, taking quick glances at each other and shrugging their shoulders. There was clearly no routine. She stomped around the stage with random demands, calling on anyone who would listen. She wore sunglasses, looking no one in the eye.

The sound check lasted two hours and fifteen minutes. At 7:15 p.m., the camera crew admitted, "You weren't joking when you said you didn't know what was going to happen." I emailed the publicist, who, to her credit, was vigilant when it came to her smartphone, asking if the interview was still a go. The show started at eight p.m. The clock was ticking. The publicist continued to say there was no way the interview would be cancelled. I was becoming exasperated, but I figured after waiting this long, we might as well wait it out.

Sure enough, a little before eight p.m., as the theater began to fill, the publicist asked us to come into the lobby. Barely making eye contact—her frigid smile now gone—she softly said, "She has to be on stage in an hour and she has to go in hair and makeup." *Wow*, I thought, *she'll even be late for the performance.*

"Does that mean we aren't going to interview her?" I asked, already knowing the answer.

"Basically—" she started, then her face dropped, "I'm sorry."

"We've waited three and a half hours," I said, "and came all the way to the Bronx—"

"I know," she replied. "Maybe we could do a phoner or an email interview."

I knew it wasn't her fault. I had already experienced the mess of this artist three years earlier. We said goodbye to the publicist and did an about face, heading back to lower Manhattan. There was no apology from the artist's camp. In all of my years interviewing, I'd never had a cancellation for an in-person interview. My experience with this artist was a representation of how some celebrities treat those who they perceive to be beneath them. The rapper was a person I promised myself I would never be, regardless of where I traveled in my career. Sadly, this rapper's lack of respect was the standard for many celebrities.

By 2014, I was working for one of the top African American online media outlets in the country, but I felt myself becoming exhausted with celebrities. I remained grateful for my career, but I needed to do more meaningful work, and interviewing celebrities about their latest project wasn't fulfilling. Yet money is crucial, and, in many ways, the work remained a dream job—how many people wouldn't want my position? However, there were two more interviews that officially took the wind out of my sails.

In October of 2014, I interviewed an up-and-coming actor on camera for a film about a pop star exhausted by fame. The movie, beautifully directed with strong performances, was a story about the toxicity of being a public figure and the ego of celebrity. Ironically, I would experience toxicity and ego in the actor I was scheduled to interview.

We sat down for a fifteen-minute interview. I asked a collection of questions about the movie, fame, Hollywood, and the craft of acting. Then, I addressed a quote I found from an earlier interview, saying he "refused to be emasculated on screen." I thought it was an interesting but short statement, considering there is ongoing dialogue about how black Americans are represented in Hollywood. As we all know, one-sentence quotes can be misleading, so I asked what he meant. Confident and casual, he answered: "Manhood is a quantifiable thing. Far too often our paths have been taken away. Whether it be physically through men who have been lynched, castrated, or from roles that have depicted black men as women or with questionable sexuality. I think it's important to make sure I present myself and my manhood as something that is everlasting—so we look to what are the representations of Hollywood now—that there's always someone there. I have kids and I think that's important. I think that's important to young men to never have to see me in lipstick or to never have to see me doing something that emasculates me, whether it be the way I present myself in an interview or the way I present myself on screen."

I was slightly confused by his response and asked a follow-up: "Does that mean you wouldn't play a gay character?"

"I don't think I would," he quickly replied. "It's a whole other conversation, but for me I've drawn my line in the sand. There's certain things to preserve the black man and what it means; I'm going to be specific to that for the rest of my career."

For years, I'd sat through conversations with stars who babbled sexism, homophobia, racism, and classism without making anyone flinch, especially in the days before social media. I accepted his opinion as just that and, in fact, knew many people would agree with him. Moreover, he appeared set in his comments, standing by his choice as an actor. We ended the interview on a positive note. He seemed genuinely pleased and happily allowed me to snap a few photos before we rode the elevator down together.

The video interview was published a week later. Several media outlets picked up his quote about avoiding gay roles to "preserve the black man," which invited split reactions. Some blasted him as homophobic; others appreciated his stance on "black manhood." A few hours after the interview began to go viral, I was flooded with emails and calls from the publicists for the film. They wanted to know why that part of the interview was included, claiming the actor told me to not include his comments. "Why would you do that to him?" one of the publicists asked, clearly chastising me. "He said he specifically told you not to include that part of the interview!"

I denied that he ever asked me for his comments to be kept off the record, saying that if the request had been made, I would've honored it. After hours of emails and calls, all remains of the content were removed from the site that published the interview. Yet, allegedly, the actor or his team pointed fingers at me, seeming to want me severely reprimanded. I was concerned I might be fired from the outlet, but my boss at the time stood by me. It's one thing to be upset that your own words earned you bad press, but to use privilege and fame to attempt to take down another black man, who doesn't possess nearly as much money and access, contradicts the pedestal of "[preserving] the black man."

I later found out the head of the studio for the film was a gay man who was offended by the comments. The actor allegedly went to their offices and apologized, backtracking by saying, "I would play James Baldwin if the role came to me!" Yeah, right. As James Baldwin once said, "I can't believe what you say, because I see what you do."

Even though the footage was removed, I was aggressively admonished by other colleagues and advised that I should distance myself from the interview, let it die down, and sidestep it if I were ever questioned about it again. "You're a black journalist," one peer said; "you have to always support black actors, no matter what they say." For the moment, I would bow my head in silence and pray the wrath of a celebrity wouldn't haunt me. I knew of talented and respected journalists who were denied access to every media event and outlet because one famous person and their team hated them. Therefore, I continued to be grateful for the career I worked so hard to build and maintained my silence.

The experience stuck with me. I came to honestly question the stability of the "be in the room with a celebrity" mentality. My job security was about celebrity access, which so often meant remaining tight-lipped. At any moment a vengeful star could decide I wasn't worthy and demolish my career. I was told to deal with any disrespect that came, because celebrities have money and power.

In August of 2015, I was assigned to interview four actors starring in a film plagued with early bad reviews—even the director claimed the film sucked. I didn't want to conduct the interviews, but the studio was convinced the lone black actor was the major sell, so they demanded "urban" press. On a blazing hot New York City day, I, along with several other journalists, dragged myself to the press junket at a glamorous hotel in Manhattan. I patiently waited for my interviews as one of my colleagues, who just finished his, whispered to me, "They clearly don't want to be here."

I sighed, "Here we go." The doors opened and I was ushered into a large hotel room, where the four actors sat facing an elaborate camera setup. The cameras started rolling as I asked several fun questions, trying my damnedest to sound optimistic about the film, which I had seen the night before. Not one question landed. The cast of millennials appeared lobotomized, mumbling under their breath, glancing at their phones. The indifference was astounding, even for me.

Yet I fought with all my journalist's might. I focused my questions on the actor I was told would be good for "urban press," but he made little eye contact and gave me extremely brief answers. Toward the end of a painful six minutes, I asked the actor about his breakout role in 2013, playing an unarmed twenty-four-year-old black man who was shot and killed by a security guard. At the time, the murder of black men by the cops was headline news, Black Lives Matter was becoming a force in politics, and the 2013 film was often referenced. "That film," I began, "we're still talking about it today considering what is happening in the country. What are your thoughts when you hear these same stories coming out affecting young black people?"

Twisting his mouth, he glared at me for a few seconds, rested his head on two fingers, and answered emptily, "I think it's sad. I think it's, umm, it's sickening. I can't give you what you want me to give right now as far as an answer...and, uh, so I'll just leave it at that."

Can't give me what I want right now? I thought. *This is the most relevant topic to the black community and it's your work!* But I thanked them for the interview and left the room.

Congregating with the other journalists, I discovered I wasn't alone. They'd all had uncomfortable experiences with him. One person vowed, "I will never interview him again." Others were getting their raw footage edited because, as one journalist told me, one of the actors "didn't like" the questions.

Studios are allowed to edit footage given to journalists, and I was nervous my footage would be scrapped. Thankfully, I was given all of my footage, but I later found out the actor, or someone in his camp, complained about me to upper management. He "didn't like" my question. My boss was shocked and sympathetic. Once again, she advocated for me. "I told upper management no one complains about you. I'm sorry you had to deal with that."

He "didn't like" my question? I thought. *It's not like I asked about his bizarre thoughts on interracial dating or misogynistic comments in interviews. I focused on his work.* In addition, I knew other black journalists who agreed to work for free to build writing credentials, as I once had, who received complaints. Unlike the actors, none of them were paid millions of dollars to attend press junkets nor did they have the perks of hair, makeup, and a luxurious hotel.

I had experienced inspirational, even life-changing interviews with Audra McDonald, Rosie Perez, Harry Belafonte, Jodie Foster, Will Smith, Ava DuVernay, and Diahann Carroll, but I was tired of the velvet rope. For every rewarding or at least respectful interview, there were several others who were wildly disappointing. I could no longer be excited about being "in the room" with a celebrity. I'm not saying these were all evil people. Maybe they were having an awful day, but celebrity culture is high maintenance. Most importantly, I resented the threat of losing my career for fear of a touchy star. I craved work that mattered.

Many people urged me not to include this essay in my book. Speaking my truth could damage my career. However, throughout my life I've been bullied into silence, and these three celebrities, and many more, time-warped me to the era of my life when I had no voice. After each of these interviews, my livelihood felt threatened, especially as a black journalist. I was basically told to hush "or else"—from publicists and managers who begged for support from black journalists, but could possibly blacklist you. The last interview may have been the moment when the documentarian in me was born. I wanted to tell the stories of the outsiders, the marginalized, those rarely seen or heard, not elitist celebrities.

So, where is the intersection? Why tell these specific stories? This is not tabloid fodder with salacious details about life behind the velvet rope. Here is why: I fought for too long to be silenced, especially by the rich, famous, and powerful. I cannot encourage people to fight back, to speak their truth, no matter how uncomfortable, if I refuse to do the same. I cannot relinquish the agency I strived for all of my life because of celebrities and classism. I will not let anyone own my voice. I did my time on that hellish road and I cannot regress, even if it means I will never sit down with another high-profile actor or performer again. This is my respect. This is my manhood. My story. You do not own me.

CORNBREAD CAKE

IN JUNE OF 2015, RACHEL DOLEZAL BECAME A HOUSEHOLD name as a white woman who was passing for black. Her story was confusing, strange, and layered with bizarre lies: she lived in a tipi, her family hunted with arrows, and she sported elaborate hairstyles she tried to pass off as "natural." Rachel wasn't "transracial;" she possessed a fetish for black culture. Rachel, who lived in Washington State like my mother and me, gave the strangest reason for why she became a race-faker. She told NBC's Matt Lauer, "I've actually had to go there with the experience, not just the visible representation, but with the experience, and the point at which that really solidified was when I got full custody of Izaiah. And he said, 'You're my real mom,' and he's in high school, and for that to be something that is plausible, I certainly can't be seen as white and be Izaiah's mom." The reason why Rachel wove a heap of outlandish lies about her racial identity was because she had a black son? This belief was seriously illogical and offensive, and I only hope Izaiah will not suffer extreme racial identity issues due to Dolezal's privileged attempt at authenticity.

I am the person I am today because my mother encouraged me to be my authentic self by remaining her authentic self. Had she spray-tanned, worn afro weaves, and insisted, "I am your black mama!", who knows how my various intersections would have manifested. My mother's affirmation of herself affirmed me as a black man with a white mother, as a gay man, and, most important, as a human being. Her standing in her truth, no matter the circumstance, helped me live my truth. Unlike Rachel, my mother never performed blackness.

"Allyship" is jargon my mother never learned, but in many ways, it describes her to a T. She wasn't a savior or some great white hope, but operated from a space of compassion. Using her street smarts, my mother taught me to approach everyone with empathy, yet never allow anyone to disrespect you. Daily, my mother marched into the war of cultural ideologies. In the battles my mother fought with the various people we met in Washington State, I saw the complex, compassionate, hateful, and willfully ignorant nuances in people of all backgrounds.

In one of our many neighborhoods in Washington State, we lived near a black Muslim family. The mother of the family, Shelia, spotted me and my mother walking down the street while she cleaned her porch. She hollered with a smile to my mother, "Hey girl, what are you doing there with that handsome little boy?" In the lily-white environment of Washington State in the 1980s, when a black person saw another black person, there was an immediate kinship, a "Who are you? Let's be friends!" reaction. For Shelia, a white woman with a black son was the closest thing to a black woman she was going to see.

"This is my son!" my mother answered proudly.

"Where are you from?" Shelia quizzed.

"Jersey!"

"Girl, I'm from Chicago!" Shelia exclaimed, as though Illinois and New Jersey were neighboring states. "Come on this porch with me and have a glass of lemonade."

My mother became close friends with Shelia, who was married with two kids. Shelia's husband was a devoted, quiet, disciplined Muslim who didn't say much but could straighten your back with one stare. One afternoon when my mother picked me up from Shelia's house, her husband said, "Julie, you have a well-behaved son and you are the only white person I will allow in my house." Shelia's eyes popped as she gasped.

"Julie, I'm sorry! He doesn't mean it in that way."

"I mean it that way," he rebutted matter-of-factly.

"It's okay, I'm the only white person I let in my house!" my mother shot back, making everyone cackle. Of course this wasn't true, but without trying my mother understood the basic mistrust some black Americans had for white people. As a white woman with a black child who she was very protective of, she developed some of that mistrust, which at times morphed into anger and acting out in dangerous and unhealthy ways.

My mother and I constantly moved around Vancouver, Washington. Living in poverty, bouncing between various resources and grappling with the latest eviction notice leaves no space for stability. Young and lacking resources, my mother was a bit of a troublemaker in her early twenties, especially with her best friend, Karla, a Mexican woman constantly disenfranchised by the racism, classism, and sexism of 1980s Washington State. Karla was the mother to two beautiful daughters and suffered in a rocky relationship with their father, who casually decided when he wanted to work, leaving Karla and her kids broke and hungry. Like my mother, Karla had little education, and the job market was scarce.

Desperate and economically bitter, Julie and Karla began stealing from "rich white people," as Karla put it. This was the height of my mother's anger toward some white people in Washington. She was disgusted by nepotism and a legacy of wealth. Still, she easily spoke the language of white folks, and Karla knew it. Their first plan connected the nuances of nationality, race, and class.

Karla and my mother loved ritzy antique stores. Due to the popularity of *Dynasty*, everyone craved a classy antique, whether or not they had the money. Julie and Karla weren't going to rob a store with weapons; they planned to use their wit. In a full, glamorous disguise (big hair, heavy makeup, and cheap clothes which they attempted to make look expensive), Karla and Julie transformed themselves into a budget Alexis Carrington and Dominique Deveraux from *Dynasty*. My mother entered the antique store first, confirmed the cashier was working alone, and proceeded to cruise for merchandise. Karla would follow behind her, staying near the front of the store. Once my mother caught Karla's eye, she'd ask for help with an item she spotted in the back of the store. My mother loved an accent (Russian, English, and Australian were a few go-tos), but her favorite was Southern.

"Excuse me, ma'am? I saw this divine vase in the back behind the glass. I would love to take a peeky-peek."

The cashier's face lit up as she exclaimed "Certainly!", ushering my mother to the back. Karla and my mother knew she had to play the role of the rich white woman to get the cashier's attention. Karla would've been dismissed. Once they were out of sight and Karla could hear my mother babbling like a Southern belle, she made her way to the cash register, which wasn't electronic and easy to pop open.

"Oh! And this vase is just the most beautiful thing. My dear pa in Alabama would love it! How much is it?"

"The vase is only eight hundred dollars!" the cashier enthusiastically responded.

"Only? What a bargain!" By this point, Karla had the old-school cash register cracked open, snatched the cash (never more than a hundred dollars), leaving only a few bills, and was moving stealthily out the door. The door opening was my mother's cue to hit the road. "Oh Lord, I must think about this some more," she said. "I'll come back later today. Thank you for all your help—and those are just lovely earrings!"

"Thank you, ma'am! Come back when you can!" As my mother strutted out of the store, Karla was perched in the driver's seat with the car running.

"Only you could pull that off," Karla laughed as they drove away. "They aren't going to believe a Mexican woman with a Southern accent."

They racked up some good cash, but these were antique stores, and the risk of getting caught was too high. Julie and Karla needed something simpler.

In those days in Vancouver, no one locked their doors, which Karla and Mom thought was asinine. Many afternoons, the Thelma and Louise of the Evergreen State casually opened the front doors of homes in the neighborhood and stole the bare necessities: food, toilet paper, bedding, toys, and money they found, never stealing anything too valuable. Still, thievery can make you lazy; they soon began opening front doors in our apartment complex, and their plan fell to pieces when Karla stole a random shower curtain. Yes, a damn shower curtain. The neighbor happened to see the shower curtain through Karla's bathroom window and flipped out, running to management.

"Karla! Now why did you steal the shower curtain?" my mother asked with a laugh. I was sprawled out on the floor in the hallway of our apartment, eavesdropping on their conversation as usual.

"I know, it was dumb. I don't know what I was thinking. It had all these beads and jewels, looked like something from *Solid Gold*! I just got greedy." They cackled, but there could be serious repercussions, especially if Karla's husband knew she had stolen a shower curtain, which could get them kicked out of the complex or result in possible jail time for Karla. "You know who can't find out. I'm scared, Julie." Karla's husband was known to beat her when he got angry. My mother surely remembered those days with my abusive father. Also, it was no secret that Karla was despised in the apartment complex for being Mexican. My mother was terrified of what might happen to Karla and her two kids.

"I'll say I did it and gave it to you," my mom decided.

"You can't do that. They'll kick you out or maybe arrest you."

"They won't arrest me. They'll arrest you. And you know why." I caught a glimpse of Karla grabbing my mother's hand and squeezing. "Are you sure you're not Mexicana?" They both laughed.

My mother told management she had stolen the shower curtain because she was drunk and gave it to Karla. They immediately kicked us out of the complex. Luckily, Karla helped my mother and me find a new home—and she lovingly stole money from her husband for our first month's rent.

Whether conscious or unconscious, my mother recognized that because she was a white woman, regardless of whether she had a black son, the apartment management would not be as hard on her. However, for Karla, there was no telling what would happen, especially at the hands of her husband. I hollered and cried when we left that apartment complex, not understanding why we moved out, but in retrospect, I am damn happy my mother took the blame for Karla.

In nearly every neighborhood we moved to in Washington State, there was a collective of racists my mother kept her eye on. Tammy was around the same age as my mother and lived a few blocks away, and they instantly clashed; their spirits just didn't mix. Tammy was a tall, lanky, loud-mouthed, boozing broad, with a cigarette perpetually in her hand and a sharp comment for anyone in earshot. Everyone hated Tammy but slightly feared her because they believed she was psychotic, with her drug dealer friends and her random shouting, threatening to kill people. My mother was not afraid.

I was no more than eight years old, but I could sense Tammy didn't like me or my mother. Although I never heard it for myself, I knew from neighborhood gossip that Tammy called me a nigger and my mother a nigger-lover. Over several months, Tammy and my mother got into several spats because of Tammy's antagonistic attitude, which usually resulted in my mother walking away. However, she never actually heard the word *nigger* uttered from Tammy's lips.

According to my mother, one day while I was at school, she was about to cross paths with Tammy on the street. They had just gotten into a heated argument the day before, and Tammy threatened to stab my mother. Tammy's go-to one-liner was, "I'll stab you, cunt!" Walking closer, my mother was on high alert as they stared each other down. When Tammy passed my mom with a Camel cigarette bouncing between her fingers, she snickered, "Nigger." My mother's rage button was finally pushed. Tammy grabbed for something in her pocket—something that appeared to be metal. My mother immediately thought she saw a knife and that Tammy might make good on her threat.

Before my mother could fully see what was coming out of Tammy's pocket, her Jersey hands were clenched around Tammy's pale throat. Mama threw Tammy on the ground, leaped on top of her, and pinned Tammy's skinny arms down with her knees, causing Tammy's shirt to bust open, exposing her breasts—Tammy never wore a bra. My mother pounded on Tammy's chest as she wailed and her long limbs flapped on the concrete. With each punch, my mother yelled, "Don't! You! Ever! Fuck! With! Me! Again!"

Mom snapped out of her rage only when Tammy's daughter ran out of the house crying uncontrollably, seeing her mother getting the ass-whooping she deserved. Mom jumped off Tammy, who was in a daze, with the cigarette still dangling between her fingers and her battered breasts exposed.

The cops were called, and the only reason my mother wasn't arrested was because everyone lied and said Tammy assaulted my mother first, but my mother decided to not press charges. Tammy didn't look my mother in the eye again, and we never heard of her calling us niggers again. Oh, and Tammy didn't have a knife in her pocket—it was an oversized metal lighter.

I'm not saying Rachel Dolezal should beat down bitches on the street like my mother did, but there was no option for my mother to be anyone but her authentic self, even if it meant violence. Thankfully, as my mother left her mid-twenties, she calmed down. One of the aunts on my father's side of the family famously told my mother, "Julie, you need to blend in more. Take it from me, as a black woman, we got to blend in. Those white folks in Washington can tell you hate them. You can't be so negative. You need them for jobs. You got to be around them for work." Essentially, my aunt was telling my mother to own her privilege and use it to play the game. To use her privilege in the way black people, especially black women, cannot. Certainly, if you are white, poor, and a single mother with a black son, your privilege is shifted, but it still exists. From that day, she began to rethink race via the intersecting journey of her son. When the time was appropriate, my mother proudly laid down the law, which was clear when it came to a teacher named Mrs. Daniel.

Mrs. Daniel's ice-blue eyes sizzled as she glared at me from the front of the class. I was in the first grade in Washington State, but my childhood innocence didn't prevent me from understanding that my teacher despised me. I couldn't piece together where her anger originated from. Although I was a chatty student, I always did my work, loved to participate, and constantly sought Mrs. Daniel's approval. I wanted her to be proud of me, but she never was.

"Take your chair and desk and move it to the back of the class!" she snapped.

"Why?" I asked softly.

"You're yawning! If the class bores you then you can sit in the back!" It was the middle of the day and I was a bit tired, like most of the students, but I wasn't falling asleep. Mrs. Daniel consistently found a reason to yell at me. I dragged my desk to the back, which made a loud screeching noise. "Stop it!" she screamed. "What's wrong with you? Just take your chair and use one of the desks in the back!"

"But you told me—"

"Just go to the back of the class!" The other children appeared uncomfortable, their eyes darting around the room, avoiding eye contact with me and Mrs. Daniel. I picked up my chair and sat in the back with my face to the wall. Mrs. Daniel continued her lesson. I tried to listen and take notes, but it was difficult to concentrate looking at a white wall. I lowered my head onto the desk and sighed. I couldn't wait to get home, I thought.

When I saw my mother, I immediately told her about Mrs. Daniel.

"She did what?" my mother asked.

"Mrs. Daniel made me face the wall for the rest of the class. She said that's where I need to sit from now on." I could see the wheels turning in my mom's mind. In seconds, she went from confusion to complete understanding.

"And why did she do this?" she calmly asked, sitting next to me and rubbing my hand. "She said I kept yawning....I don't know."

"Has anyone else in your class sat in the back with their face to the wall?" my mother quizzed.

"No..."

My mother grabbed the phone and quickly dialed. "Yes, this is Julie Jones and my son is in Mrs. Daniel's class....The African American boy? Yes, that's him, the only African American in the class." I recognized the controlled anger in my mother's voice. "I need to see the principal first thing tomorrow morning....This is urgent. I need to see the principal tomorrow, and if I don't, I'm going to the school board....Yes, I can hold on." My mother gave me a soft smile. "Yes, I'm here....Okay, my son and I will be there." She hung up. "I'm going with you to school tomorrow and we're going to take care of this," she told me. "Come on, sit down next to Mommy." I sat by her on the couch as she embraced me.

"You know how I've told you sometimes people are going to treat you differently because of the color of your skin?"

"Yeah," I said, nodding.

"Well, this is one of those times," she said. I understood. There was a feeling from Mrs. Daniel that I couldn't immediately translate into words as a child, but I trusted my mother. She was never wrong about people.

"So what do we do?" I asked.

"I'm going to handle it. But I need you to know, your mother isn't going to always be here. One day, and that day might come sooner than later, you're going to be by yourself and deal with people who will think it's okay to treat you different."

"Why are people like that?"

"They've been taught the wrong things. When you've been taught the wrong things for so long sometimes it's hard to do the right things."

"Mommy, I'm glad you were taught the right things," I said. My mother paused.

"Well, I wasn't, but something in me knew it was wrong to treat anyone different. And you gotta remember that adults don't always get it right. If you make anyone feel bad, no matter what or who they are, then you gotta treat them better. People should feel happy around you. No one should feel the way you felt around Mrs. Daniel. Understand?" I nodded.

The next morning, my mother marched into my elementary school holding my little hand and walking with such speed I could barely keep up. We arrived an hour before class specifically for this meeting. She swung open the doors to the school's office, startling the frail secretary. "Oh, my! You scared me," the secretary gasped.

"My son and I are meeting with Principal Rodgers and Mrs. Daniel."

"What time?" the secretary questioned.

"Now," my mother responded coldly.

"Hold on." The secretary slowly walked to another room, keeping her gaze focused on my mother.

"You just let me do all the talking. I'm going to handle this. And I want you to pay attention. You can't let anyone disrespect you. I'm here now, but you're going to be a big boy one day and you need to know how to stand up for yourself." I quickly nodded. My mother was a soldier, a warrior, and the strongest person I knew. When she gave orders, I paid attention.

The secretary motioned to us, her steely eyes still set on my mother. We entered Principal Rodgers's office, Mrs. Daniel was seated by a window, far from the two empty chairs where my mother and I would sit. Principal Rodgers greeted my mother with an awkward handshake, but didn't say a word to me. He was a short, chubby, elderly man with a bald head and a belly stretching out his tight shirt, the buttons hanging on for dear life. I rarely saw him, and this was my first time in his office, which was flooded with paperwork and stank of leather. Mrs. Daniel gave a slight nod to my mother, her lips tight, face motionless, and hands cupped on her lap.

Principal Rodgers plopped in his chair, causing papers to fall, as my mother and I sat down. He began, "Mrs. Jones, I know there have been some disciplinary problems with your son."

"Disciplinary problems?" my mother questioned, leaning toward him. "There are no disciplinary problems. My son is an A student. I have never had a disciplinary problem with my son. If there was a disciplinary problem then I should've been told sooner."

"Mrs. Jones," Principal Rodgers said, putting his hands up and giving a goofy smile. "Your son is a good boy. Mrs. Daniel is a good teacher and—"

"I want to know why Mrs. Daniel put my child in the back of the class with his face to the wall," my mother interrupted. Principal Rodgers shot eyes at Mrs. Daniel.

"Mrs. Daniel, did you put him in the back of the class with his face to the wall?" he questioned, sounding confused.

"Oh, she didn't tell you?" my mother added, slightly rolling her neck and turning to Mrs. Daniel.

"Did you?" Principal Rodgers asked again.

"Yes," Mrs. Daniel replied, still stone-faced.

"Why?" Principal Rodgers nicely asked.

"He was being disruptive," she flatly answered.

"And why are you always so rude to my son? My son told me you snap at him. Yell at him. Why?" I heard the anger rising in my mother's tone.

Mrs. Daniel paused, only making eye contact with Principal Rodgers. "Shouldn't the child be in another room? I don't think it's appropriate for him to be here."

"It's very appropriate for my son to be here to see exactly the type of person you are," my mother stated.

Finally, Mrs. Daniel locked eyes with my mother. "Excuse me?" she said. There was a strange quiet that dragged for what felt like minutes; the tension between the two of them boiled. My mother didn't blink, burning the teacher with her stare. Mrs. Daniel huffed, glanced quickly at me, and turned back to Principal Rodgers. "This is ridiculous."

"You're treating my son this way because he's black," my mother spat. Mrs. Daniel let out a heavy gasp, putting her hand to her chest.

Principal Rodgers nearly fell out of his wobbly chair, "Mrs. Jones! Please! Mrs. Daniel has been a teacher here for twenty-five years and no one has ever called her a racist!"

"You know what? I didn't even say the word *racist,* but that's a better word. She's a racist." Principal Rodgers's jaw dropped like my mother had babbled Satanic chants. Mrs. Daniel's hands were back on her lap, cupped so tight I thought she might break her skin. My mother's conviction overpowered the room as she made eye contact with the both of them. The two white educators had never experienced a woman like my mother. She spoke with a husky East Coast accent from New Jersey; she was a twenty-five-year-old single mother with—most importantly—a black son. We were aliens to them and they were clueless to their bias. My mother may not have known the language, but she knew the feeling of microaggressions.

Her objective in the moment was to affirm me as a black child, the only one in the room. She knew it was her job, as a mother, to affirm that I existed in reality. Sometimes "the talk" on race isn't enough; sometimes you need to see the action. "How many black students has Mrs. Daniel taught?" my mother grilled. Principal Rodgers and Mrs. Daniel exchanged glances. "How many?"

"It doesn't matter how many black students she's taught," Principal Rodgers stammered. "She's a professional."

"Mrs. Daniel," my mother said, facing her. "How many students have you put in the back of the class with their face to the wall?" Mrs. Daniel was burning with raw hate, face flushed and hands still cupped in her lap.

"I can't believe you're making this about color," Mrs. Daniel hissed through clenched teeth, stressing the word "color."

"How many?" my mother repeated, aggressive but calm.

"Mrs. Jones, calm down!"

"I *am* calm, Principal Rodgers. Do you really think this is the first time I've experienced this?"

"Mrs. Daniel," he said, ignoring the last comment from my mother. "Have you ever disciplined a child in that way?"

Mrs. Daniel huffed again, looking at me, then back at her boss. "No, I haven't."

"This woman is a racist," my mother declared again with a sigh.

"You're getting way out of line, Mrs. Jones," Principal Rodgers barked, attempting to be aggressive.

"You know what's way out of line? The fact that I walked into this school today with my son and neither the secretary, nor you, nor Mrs. Daniel said one word to him." Principal Rodgers's eyes bulged. "And let me tell you something, Mrs. Daniel," my mother continued, "I know you. I've been around people like you all my life." She paused, her eyes burning into Mrs. Daniel's face. "*I see you.* I see you for exactly who you are. You aren't going to fool me. Whatever issue you have with me or my son, it's going to stop today." She turned back to Principal Rodgers. "I want my son out of her class today or my next stop is the school board. I'll sit there all day if I have to."

Principal Rodgers gave up. I was placed in another class. My mother met the teacher first. She was a much younger woman, a first-year teacher, and extremely cheerful. I don't know what was said during that discussion, but the new teacher greeted me with open arms. Every day my mother asked about school, but the question came with a different connotation. Like any parent, my mother shielded me from racism, but this moment was one I needed to experience, because I had met and would meet many more Mrs. Daniels in my life. After a certain age, I didn't need my mother to stomp down to the school. I was my mother's child and prepared for the unavoidable truths.

My mother wasn't perfect, and maybe there were other ways to handle all of these situations, but she never forgot compassion. As a white woman with diverse friends and family, she was embraced because she stayed rooted in her true self. Whether you are around Mexicans, Muslims, blacks, or whites, you can only march in as yourself and no one else, from a place of empathy and understanding.

By the time I was a teenager, my mother and father decided I should permanently move to Philadelphia. I felt anger and rejection. As we know, the complexities of life are clearer in hindsight. One of my mother's greatest fears was that I would have no connection to my culture as a black man. Yes, she walked in her truth, but she knew, because of her own empathy, that she could only teach me so much in an environment like Washington. I needed my own community, my culture, regardless of the struggles to come.

On October 18, 1991, my mom walked my fourteen-year-old self onto the Greyhound bus for a four-day ride (of course we couldn't afford the luxury of a flight). She hugged me tighter than I could ever remember and sobbed mommy tears: "You don't know how hard it is for me to let you go." If my heart could've bled in that moment, it would have.

"I don't wanna go," I mumbled, tears choking my throat.

"You have to go. This is the right thing to do. I know it is. It's time for you to be with your father. Not forever, but for now. This is only tempo-rary." She cupped my face in her hands. Her eyes were gray and my eyes were brown, but I had my mother's eyes. Her lips were thinner, mine were fuller, but I had my mother's smile. I felt our history in her touch, the mistakes, the laughs, the music, the food, the tears, all the ebbs and flows of parent and child. She did the best with what she knew. She was a phenomenal mother.

"Ma'am, we have to go," the bus driver groaned. We separated. She walked down the bus aisle as I collapsed into my seat. The doors closed; I heard the wheels of the bus turning. I tapped on the window; she spotted me and made the "I love you" sign with her fingers. I gave her the "I love you" sign back. I kept my eye on her as she stood like a statue, holding up the "I love you" sign. The bus turned the corner and she vanished. I must have cried for an hour on that bus.

As we drove deeper into Washington, I saw an advertisement for Jiffy cornbread and began to smile and giggle uncontrollably. My birthday was April 26, always the end of the month when we had no food or money. Dur-ing the roughest years, she scraped together enough cash to buy two boxes of Jiffy cornbread mix. She'd whip together the cornbread and add a touch of vanilla extract, cinnamon, and nutmeg. She'd fill the cake pans with Jiffy and let it bake; our small apartment would be permeated with the sweetness of my soon-to-be birthday cake. Within thirty minutes, the two layers were slapped together with a thick layer of chocolate frosting, or whatever frosting we had. She'd write with the frosting, "Happy birthday, Mommy loves you the whole wide world." The memory calmed me. She always made something out of anything with no shame. Nothing made me happier on those birthdays. Jiffy cornbread cake baked with love by my mother is still the best birthday cake I've ever had.

KILLING
MY FATHER

"I WANT TO BE A GIRL" IS THE FIRST SENTENCE I REMEMBER saying to my father. His eyes widened, his face contorted, and his jaw tightened. With those six words, he instantly abandoned his son.

Most of my early memories of my father begin with violence. My mother, exhausted, bruised and terrified, sitting on the floor, leaning up against a wall, long hair framing her face, repeating, "He's gonna kill me. He's gonna kill me." Soon after, we were on a Greyhound bus from California to live with her mother in Washington State. As an adult, I've attempted to reimagine my father's propensity to control, strike, and abuse. Part of this rage is not his fault. He was a black man raised in the 1960s and 1970s, grappling with black masculinity, and clearly taught by generations before him that upholding his so-called manhood was crucial to his survival.

I was the opposite of what he defined as manhood: sensitive, feminine, and more brain than brawn. Parents envision dreams for their child. I was the son he never wanted, which he couldn't control and I couldn't change.

I was born Tyrone Clay, Jr. I hated that my mother named me after him. Without the language to explain, I longed for my own identity. Why did she name me after a man who abused her and everything around him? He was not the man I wanted to be. My mother explained, "I thought the name sounded strong. I wanted you to have a strong name." Throughout school, when teachers called me by my father's name, I winced. As a child, I asked to be called Conrad, a name I picked up from watching *G.I. Joe*, but my mother refused. At the start of the seventh grade I was beginning at a new school in a different district, so I introduced myself to everyone as T.C. My mother abhorred the nickname, but I was proud to find another version of myself. T.C. didn't go over well. The vicious kids bullied me to death for being black and effeminate. I was quickly labeled "T. She." I can laugh about it today, but it hurt like hell when I was a kid.

My mother's relationship with my father was complicated. She escaped him and didn't want him in her life, but being that she was raised fatherless, she felt it was important for me to have a connection with him and his family. After long conversations with my aunts (my father's sisters), they agreed it was healthy for me to know my father. I began visiting him during the summer. First for a month in the summer of 1986. But in June of 1987, my father wanted me to spend the full summer with him.

I was ten years old and my father was living in California with his girlfriend, Paula. My father, who was twenty-nine at the time, begged my mother to let me stay with him for the entire summer. Although he would never admit it, I think he was concerned with the femininity he had seen in me the year before—perhaps more time with him could "butch" me up.

She was hesitant, but he pushed. I was his son. I "needed" a man around me. He argued he wasn't the violent man he used to be when they dated in their late teens and early twenties. Also, my father planned to move back to Philadelphia during the summer, so we would have the opportunity to drive cross-country from California to Philadelphia, some father-son bonding. My mother eventually agreed.

My father drove from Sacramento, California, to Vancouver, Washington, with Paula. I could see the nervousness in my mother's eyes. She hadn't seen him in years. They gave each other an awkward hello. The power dynamics of their relationship were gone. My mother felt nothing for him, but she didn't want me to be an adult man who never knew his dad. She would let me decide if I needed him in my life.

Sacramento was fun the first few weeks—swimming pools and nonstop sun—but my father and I clashed. The words "I want to be a girl" rang in his brain. He would grill me: "You remember saying that, don't you?" I shook my head no, but I remembered vividly. I couldn't explain why I'd said it. I was playing with gender, not categorically defining myself. "Well, you can't be a girl, because that would make you a faggot, get it?" my dad explained combatively. I nodded, sensing his exhaustion. He didn't want a faggot son. It wasn't about me; a faggot son represented his own failure as a man.

I loved his girlfriend, Paula. She was kind, never judged me, and would often bicker with my father about how aggressive he was with me. Paula and my dad argued constantly. I was just one of many hot-button topics. Day by day, the tension grew. A week before we were about to leave for our cross-country trip to Philadelphia, my father and Paula were screaming at each other in the kitchen of her small apartment. I was balled up on the couch, my insides twisted, overwhelmed by their yelling. Paula was hysterical, hands shaking, face red, demanding my father get away from her. He was moving in closer, softly pushing and telling her to shut up. Paula was crying and covering her face with her hands. "Leave her alone, Dad," I pleaded. He ignored me, as Paula shot me a pitiful look; fear seized her face as my father's ego spread like fire, consuming everything in sight. She forcibly pushed him away, almost making him fall. Like he'd been waiting for the push, my father tightened his lip and punched Paula squarely in the face. The sound of his fist striking her face shot through the room. I screeched and my mind raced. I was transported to my first memory of my father beating the daylights out of my mother. Paula's primal scream brought me back to the apartment in Sacramento. I was sobbing.

"See? Look what you made me do! You made me hit you in front of my son!" My father looked at me, his hands up, shaking his head. "This is your fault!" he yelled at her. Paula pushed him again and he finally let her go. She grabbed her purse, running out of the house. My memory goes blank after that moment, but I never saw Paula again. I assumed she waited until my father and I left California to return.

When I spoke to my mother, I never told her what happened between my father and Paula. He stood by the phone, arms crossed as his eyes burned into me. I was sworn to secrecy. No one could scare me like my father. I was silent. To this day, he has never addressed or admitted to punching Paula, my mother, or any other woman.

Maybe because I was a child, I pushed the violence from my father into the deepest recesses of my ten-year-old soul. I had seen my mother assaulted by other men. I saw neighbors or people on the street—all women—abused by men. Sadly, my father's violence was normal. Furthermore, we were about to embark on a weeklong trip across the country; there was no escaping him. Like so many children, I compartmentalized my father into his actual self and his parental self.

For the next week, my father and I traveled cross-country from Sacramento to Philadelphia in his red Nissan 300ZX. Ironically and surprisingly, especially after the abuse I'd seen from him less than a week earlier, the trip is my best memory with my dad—just him and me on the road, riding through America. My father was ashamed of me, especially during our time in Sacramento, when he began to realize I was not going to change. But on the road together, father and son cooped up in his sports car, he unclenched his hypermasculine ego. There was no one eyeing us to question his manhood. He was the most relaxed I had ever seen him.

He laughed and smiled, two things I rarely saw him do. He told me stories about growing up in Philly, how he was inspired to become a boxer after seeing Muhammad Ali on television, and G-rated tales of serving in the Navy. He passed on fatherly lessons only seen in sitcoms: "Be early for everything. If you're right on time, you're late." "Always do what you say you'll do. A real man is dependable." "Save your money. I don't care if you get four quarters; you save two of them." "It ain't always about race and color, I've been around all types of people, but don't ever forget you're black. The minute you forget it, somebody will remind you." My father wasn't forward-thinking enough to challenge his violence, emotional abuse, and toxic masculinity, but these were his lessons.

He even allotted me some freedom to be a child. When Madonna's "Who's That Girl?", which was the song of the summer, played on the radio, he allowed me to listen every time. When I reenacted scenes from *The Bionic Woman*, he didn't say I was acting like a faggot. I was able to move the way I felt without him groaning. It was okay for me to babble, although before the trip he would holler, "Only girls talk that much!" I talked for hours on the road, keeping him awake.

We rode through every state as I read a gargantuan road map that was nearly as big as my ten-year-old body. My father was awestruck by my reading skills. "Boy, you can read! How can you read all those words at ten?"

"I don't know," I said, shrugging.

"Your mother did right raising you in Washington. That's why you can read like that," my father resolved, more to himself than me. My map-reading skills had us driving up the steep mountains of Colorado, which was the shortest route. My father suffered a fear of heights, but wanted to get to Philly as fast as possible, and avoiding the mountains would give us another day on the road. As we slowly drove through the heavenly mountains at high altitude, my father began to hyperventilate, struggling with the car.

"It's okay, Dad," I assured him, not even slightly bothered by the altitude.

"It's almost over, the road is gonna go down soon. The map says it right here," I pointed, holding the map up. "See?" He nodded, hands gripping the steering wheel.

As the road descended, and he breathed, my daddy acknowledged, "You got me through that one, son." As complicated as my father was at the time, I was grateful my mother allowed me to go with him for that experience alone. Our road trip was one of the few moments when I felt love from him.

Back in Philadelphia, my father was on a mission to make me a man. He dragged me to his local gym for boxing lessons. He'd wrap my terrified little hands in boxing gloves and push me into the ring with a boy my size. I was no fighter and, embarrassingly, missed every punch, but every one of the boy's punches landed on me. The blows only felt like taps, but the disappointment in my father's eyes was more painful. The coach, an elderly man with a thick gray beard who was a mentor to my dad when he was a teenager, would give me lectures. My father stood with his arms crossed, head nodding. "Listen, young man, you can't walk around here acting like some sugarfoot. Are you a man?" the coach grilled, pointing at my heart.

"Yeah."

"Well, then you gotta act like one. Walk straight. Don't be moving your hands all over the place. Make your voice deeper. You can't be no pussy. You got it?" I nodded. This was my first time absorbing the performance of masculinity. I needed to act. It didn't matter if it was real; the purpose was to convince others of my manhood before it was questioned. That summer was the lesson in my father's version of being a man. I was happy to return to Washington at the end of August.

By the time I was fourteen, my mother and I were struggling deeply. She was in a new relationship, fighting alcoholism, and, in many ways, knew I needed to be around my father and his family. No more summer visits—by October of 1991, I was permanently living with my dad and he tried (again) to convert me to full-blown manhood. My mother encouraged me to be my unconventional self, so when I arrived in Philadelphia, I had long, curly hair that I'd attempted to dye blonde, but had ended up a strange orange color. Quickly, my father took me to the barber shop and cut off all my hair. I held back crying in the chair while he stared, ready to rage if a single tear dropped.

I was very effeminate, and he was dedicated to purging the femme out of me. Whenever I made an effeminate movement or sound, he snapped his fingers, like a master training his dog. "Every time I snap, it means you're acting like a girl," he explained. His snaps made me jump, causing endless anxiety as I prayed to go a day without hearing a snap. If I talked, walked, or moved against his standard of masculinity after several snaps, he would rage on me: "Stop acting like a faggot! Stop it! You keep acting like this, you're going to grow up and get fucked by men! Is that what you want?" I became seriously introverted. I was afraid to speak or move too suddenly and was in a state of constant nervousness. There was no space to be myself. I was labeled a "nervous child," but no one understood that my father kept me on a choking, hypermasculine leash. I'd practice masculinity in the mirror. Trying to move my hands the "right" way, pacing my steps so I wasn't "swishing"; studying masculinity was my survival technique to endure the mental abuse from my father.

The horrors of high school in Philadelphia were countless, but I managed to reinvent myself with a new name—Clay. It was fitting; I saw a piece of myself in the name, but it was separate from my father. Despite getting notes in school reading "Clay, are you gay?", I was happy with another version of myself, and my father made no mention of it. However, he wanted to see a girlfriend in his fifteen-year-old son's life. When I finally landed a girlfriend, he said, "If your girlfriend wants to stay the night, she can. She can say she's staying with one of her friends. I won't tell her mother. Ain't nothing wrong with you having a girl in your bed." My father was so consumed with my sexuality that he was willing to allow a fourteen-year-old girl and a fifteen-year-old boy to sleep in the same bed to hopefully rescue my heterosexuality. My girlfriend never stayed the night, but we spent several days after school alone in my bedroom, with my father in the living room, probably praying her vagina would convert me.

For a little over a year, I moved back to Washington, but after feuding with my mother's boyfriend, I was back in Philadelphia in June of 1994. I was seventeen, my voice dropped, and I was nearly a man, having successfully taught myself enough masculinity to not be called "faggot" as a senior in high school. However, after I met my best friend Nikki, who sensed the gay on me, she invited me to attend an LGBT youth meeting in Center City, Philadelphia. I finally met young people of color, like myself, who were grappling with similar struggles. In March of 1995, I found my tribe.

One of the members of the youth meeting gave me James Earl Hardy's

B-Boy Blues, a book about a black gay man in New York City struggling with dating and love. Accidentally, I left the book on my bed, and my father saw the cover. He would regularly come to my room when I wasn't home to sniff out any secret homo trinkets. The book slipped my mind.

When I arrived home after school, he stopped me, face flushed, eyes bloodshot, and a hot anger in his voice. "I saw that faggot book on your bed." My heart skipped. "I'll have a murderer in my house, I'll have a drug dealer in my house, but I won't have no faggot in my house. And don't wear any of my pants, because I don't want no blood on them." I still shake my head in confusion at that last comment. To this day, I'll never understand why bloody anal sex came to my father's mind.

In June of 1995, at eighteen years old, I graduated from high school. The summer of 1995 changed my life; I was on the streets at all hours, rarely home, sleeping on any one of my friends' couches. Once I discovered my people, I shedded my struggles with sexuality. There was camaraderie amongst my friends; none of us wanted to exist in hellish environments where we weren't loved. We were the unwanted, and we bonded. Although my grandfather would say, "You know your father loves you," love doesn't matter if you don't feel it. Love is not something you know; love is what you feel.

In December of 1995, I met my first love. Like most firsts, it was passionate and quick. By June of 1996, we were moving in together, and I was ecstatic. I didn't want to live with my father a millisecond longer, and moving across the country to be in Washington State with my mother wasn't an option. I found my people, and my first love, in Philly—the city was my home. I wanted freedom from both of my parents.

My father was furious that I was moving out. I thought he'd be overjoyed to have his faggot son out of the house, but, as with his relationships with women, he wanted to maintain complete control. I believe he enjoyed trying to destroy me, and it angered him that I wouldn't shatter. My mother gave me a shield of confidence; she was affectionate, kind, and rooted in love. My father was stuck in his constructs, which again, was not solely his fault. No one told him any different, but I needed to escape him. The father I knew during our road trip across America eight years earlier was a father I had rarely seen since.

For the new apartment with my boyfriend—my father did not know who I was moving in with—all I owned was a small television, a full-size bed, and a dresser. I kindly asked my father if I could bring those three items with me.

Arms crossed, sitting in his favorite recliner, he responded, "No! I bought it. That's my stuff."

"Can I at least take the bed?"

"No! No! No! All you can take are your clothes—that's it." I stared at him, my hate seething. I didn't see myself in this man. I despised his face, words, and mannerisms, everything that made him. I couldn't understand how any woman ever loved him. I couldn't understand how he treated people so awfully, yet always came out on top. It was as if he'd made a deal with the devil. "Why are you looking at me like that?" he roared.

"I don't understand why you are so mean...I'll be sure to move out while you are at work," I confirmed, heading to the door, ready to spend the night at the new place with my boyfriend. In twenty-four hours, all remains of me would be gone.

"You ain't shit, nigga!" he yelled. "You can't make it out there. You're weak! You ain't even as strong as your mother. Six months!" I opened the door, with his voice trailing behind me. "I give you six months out there and you'll be right back here!"

I saw my boyfriend parked on the street, waiting for me in his car with a smile on his face. My soul warmed. The realization that I was going from infinite hostility to respectful love calmed me. I softly closed the door to my father's house, hate, and abuse.

I lasted longer than six months. In fact, I never returned. For years, my father and I didn't speak. However, after I moved to the New York City area in my early twenties, he attempted to get closer to me. He would visit, but I found myself falling into the same old paranoia from my teenage years. I was attempting to de-gay my apartment, hiding anything that didn't represent heterosexuality.

But at twenty-four, I had enough. I told him I was gay, and he responded with, "Well, I always knew you were haywire, being up under your mother like that for so many years." I shut down again.

Several years went by and my father married a woman who I easily bonded with. She made a valiant effort to reconnect us. For several years, our relationship was healthy. We never mentioned my sexuality, that was the invisible boundary, but when my career started to take off, our reconciliation backfired. In 2009, I interviewed Mary J. Blige, and my father was floored. I believe it was the first time he understood what I was doing with my life in New York City. A few months later, when I arrived at his house for Thanksgiving and walked into the dining room, I was shocked to see an eight-by-ten framed photo of Mary and me on the wall, overlooking our holiday dinner. I remembered emailing him the photo, but I couldn't believe he had gotten it printed and framed. I thought, *Maybe my father is proud of me.*

Later that evening, he asked me all about the interview, and before I could get to the part where I thanked her for *My Life*, my dad questioned, "You don't tell people that you are funny, do you?"

"Funny?" I repeated.

"Yeah, you know. You shouldn't tell people that. Someone like Mary J. Blige might not want someone talking to her who is funny like that." I lowered my head and took a deep breath. I wasn't in the mood to argue.

"What did I do now?" he stammered with his hands up. I walked away. I wouldn't allow him to tarnish my memory with Mary.

As my career grew, he enjoyed the glow of watching me on television interviewing celebrities, but when my work became more political and addressed equality, especially on LGBT issues, his embarrassment about me returned. His wife told me that if I ever discussed anything LGBT on any network, he refused to watch.

When my documentary *Holler If You Hear Me: Black and Gay in the Church* was released in 2015, my father was silent. On February 24, 2016, the film was featured at the White House for Black History Month. I invited several people from my family, including my father's wife, but not him. He never acknowledged the film, never watched the film, and I didn't think he'd be comfortable at the White House with his faggot son. My father went into a rage—that I only heard about secondhand—because he wasn't invited. His wife warned me, "Your father is really upset he wasn't invited to the White House. If he texts you, please ignore him."

I told her, "You tell him that if he has the nerve to text me, expect the wrath of several decades on him. He will not ruin this moment for me with his negativity." I was shocked that he wouldn't acknowledge one of the greatest accomplishments of my career until I was honored by the White House. *He's my father,* I thought. *He needs to love me not only when I'm in the light, but when I'm in the shadows.*

In college, I read *Cane* by Jean Toomer, published in 1923, about a mixed-race man who travels down South to find his roots. The story was unconventional, spiritual, beautiful, and centered on rediscovery. I saw myself in the characters, language, and vignettes of *Cane*: Rhobert, Calling Jesus, and Blood-Burning Moon. *Cane* became my daily handbook, grappling with the concepts of intersectionality decades before the term existed. When I read the line, "Call them from their houses, and teach them to dream," I dreamed of owning my identity.

I fought all my life not to be my father. He represented unflinching patriarchy, misogyny, violence, homophobia, and ultra-masculinity. I despised the idea of becoming a writer and having his name attached to the stories, narratives, and thoughts I created. I was mortified at the thought of appearing on television with "Tyrone Clay" under my face. I cringed at anyone acknowledging me with his name or his identity. I dreamed of dismantling my father from my dreams. I did not want my history tied to him. Moreover, he would not want his name connected with the identities I embraced and he rejected.

I could not tolerate his name following me like an affliction. Sure, I could dissect the nuances of black manhood, how my father was raised, how my grandfather was raised, and how my great-grandfather was raised. However, a child cannot process the historical, political, and intellectual reasons he felt unloved.

In 2007, without my father's knowledge, I officially changed my name to Clay Cane. I dismembered Tyrone Clay from my legacy, deracinating his roots from mine. In killing my father from my future, I ended his cycle of abuse and created the best version of myself.

Yes, I survived my father, but in fragile moments, his voice continues to gnaw at me. At low points, I've struggled to shrug off his toxic words, monstrous presence, and seething anger. How different would my life be if my father encouraged me to exist as myself? Going beyond my father, I also can't dismiss the residue of poverty, losing friends to HIV, the blows of words like *nigger* and *faggot*, or surviving spiritual violence. This is not a tale of "I moved on and now I'm fabulous!" We carry the past and the present. The scars of our past are a piece of our intricate imperfections. These experiences not only form who we are; they shape our fears and burdens. That's the other part of intersections—they're not solely the identities, they're the fights we may never win, which are unavoidable in the journey.

My father insisted my identities remain secret. In spite of his demons, fully embracing my labels, even with discomfort, allowed me to unearth my voice from wreckage. I fought to flourish in a world that didn't accept me.

My greatest lessons manifested from the individuals who were least like me, including my father. Would I have been as resilient if it weren't for my complicated father? Had I remained blind to the nuances of friends, family, lovers, or strangers, I would've lost a lifetime of lessons. As I forge ahead into war every day, there is no guarantee I won't face bias, but I have lived through enough to be prepared for the battlefield.

ABOUT THE AUTHOR

 **CLAY CANE** is an award-winning journalist, author, and television personality. He is the creator and director of the original documentary *Holler If You Hear Me: Black and Gay in the Church,* which earned a 2016 GLAAD Media Award nomination for Outstanding Digital Journalism. He is also the recipient of the Gay Men of African Descent's 2016 James Baldwin Revolutionary Award. Raised in both Washington State and Philadelphia, Clay's diverse background inspires him to deliver edgy commentary that provides sharp, witty, incisive, and raw analysis on culture. For more information, visit claycane.net.

Photo: J.S. Harrington